GO SELL MY BUSINESS

Editor: Ronnie Ajoku (on beha
Journal)

1st Edition Printed November 2022

ISBN: 978-1-7392311-0-1

BUS015000 Mergers & Acquisitions

BUS063000 Strategic Planning

BUS066000 Training

A copy of this book is available at the British Library.

This book is dedicated to:

Mark's Dedication

This book is dedicated to my Princess who has put up with me working weekends and late nights putting this book together. It is also dedicated to all the hard-working business owners that have dedicated their lives to building businesses, creating products, providing valuable services and creating jobs.

Adrian's Dedication

Writing this dedication, it is as if there is a person on each of my shoulders. I am reminded that as an entrepreneur, our education only really begins when we leave school and then, unless you get educated and take massive action it could all have been in vain. And a big thank you to Zena for removing my ability to waste hours procrastinating. I still have the ringing in my ears - "Just get it done!" Thanks.

Introduction

You have put blood, sweat and years into your business and you have now got to the point where you are thinking of selling it. Congratulations on picking up this book, which will help you navigate the final pieces of the puzzle you need to know (and do) before you sail off into the sunset. (*Buying a boat is optional*).

Even if you decide now is not the right time to sell your business, this book will help you understand the value of your business and make sure you understand the process and have prepared all the information necessary to facilitate a smooth sale.

Whilst you might make a good living from your business, you only really make money on your business when you exit!

That said, I will always advocate that now is always the right time. In fact, a good friend of mine has a mantra, "the best time to sell your business is now".

Reading this book will give you a good understanding of what your life's work is worth. Thoroughly understanding that value early will allow you to add more vale to it, making the business more attractive to a buyer.

Throughout the book you will hear real third-party stories of deals that went well and deals that didn't go well, enabling you to learn lessons from us and our vast network of Mergers & Acquisition professionals from around the world.

You will also get the answers to questions you might have such as: "I am an entrepreneur and an SME business owner, why do I need to know the value of my business?" for example.

Great question and you are missing a trick. The reason to know the value is that some Business owners look at their business as a pension pot and will build it until they want out, sell and retire.

- Issues – never sold a business before
- You cannot afford to screw it up!
- What is it worth – can you afford to retire?

Like a pension you need a regular, at least annual review. Is it going where you want? Does your strategy need to change, or do you need to work longer? Or can you order the Sunseeker yacht and retire to Monaco? (*Don't do it, don't buy a boat*)

Some businesses will look to grow organically or via an M&A strategy. By understanding the value of your own business, you can value others. Are they cheap - buy, expensive - walk away.

By understanding the value of your business, you can take a step back and look at it objectively, then decide what needs to change or be worked on to realise your goals.

When you do decide to sell you don't want some business broker blowing sunshine up your arse and telling you it will sell in four weeks, that you will get an unrealistic multiple and the payment will all be in cash. In this guide you will understand why they do this and the little value they actually bring to the table.

If you can find or get approached for a takeover, you have done your homework and can have a more meaningful conversation.

Even though you might not think you are prepared to sell your business, you can still have the conversation. This guide will help you to fill in the blanks in the process for when you are ready to close the sale and exit. Build a business that someone would be prepared to buy

Within this book there are links to access a number of templates that you will find useful in preparing and selling your business.

Carpe diem, go sell your business. Now read how…

NB: Names have been changed to protect the innocent, the not so innocent and the infamous...

PART I: Where to Start

Like most entrepreneurs, you have been running a business successfully but have probably never sold one before. This will all be new territory for you. It will be the most important sale you will ever make, so understanding what a buyer is looking for is paramount to getting the sale agreed and closed (in anticipation of the boat brochure landing on your doormat).

There are two important considerations you should take into account when you start thinking about selling.

Firstly, you need to think about who you can ask for advice and information and the order in which you do so is crucial. But how are most people supposed to know? The honest answer is they do not.

If you decided to sell your business today, who would be the first professional advisor you would call to discuss it? Your accountant? Your lawyer? That is almost certainly a big mistake.

You know these people and you trust them so why not ask them for advice? To answer this question, let us look at it from a slightly different perspective. You wouldn’t go to your travel agent for advice on buying your dream boat even though you trusted them to book your last cruise. You would go to Sunseeker or Princess. It might by sailing but they have a very specific areas of expertise. It's the same with businesspeople. Most lawyers, for example, do not have the resources or expertise needed to value a business, nor do they have the experience to market a business to investors, negotiate with multiple buyers and finally close the sale with the best buyer.

Although some accounting and law firms have established mergers and acquisitions departments to assist their clients, they are relatively rare and are usually geared towards catering to very large corporates. So, your lawyer may be very good at providing the legal advice needed to run your business, but in most cases he or she does not have the tools, knowledge and experience to develop, implement and execute a strategy for the optimal sale of your business. That is the work of specialists, and most law firms are simply not set up to do that. You can often find that your lawyer may be able to put together the legal due diligence documents for a prospective buyer, but outside of that my experience has been they get in the way and often destroy deals as they don't understand M&A law which is very different from writing letters to collect debt. It is the same with your accountant, they are probably one of thousands of practices who are setup to produce your end-of-year accounts and file your tax returns. Your accountant may not have even given your business financial advice over the many years you have been with them; they probably don't have the skills required either. They will probably be able to put together your financial due diligence but that is where it should end. Both accountants and lawyers practice very specific areas for the services they provide. It would be like going to see an optician for brain surgery and you wouldn't do that would you.

I once worked on a deal for a small business in the recruitment sector with a turnover of £1.2m and £100k of profits. The owner had accepted the offer of £300k, the deal was structured, the heads of terms signed, and the share purchase agreement signed. When the owner took the information to his accountant to make the changes at Companies House in the UK, his accountant told him he could get him a valuation for the business based on a multiple of 8x and that he should back out of the deal that was on the table. What happened here was the accountant had previously worked on a due diligence deal for a £30m turnover business, which was a strategic deal that had a much higher multiple than those typically applied to a small business and a financial buyer would ever achieve. We explain more about the difference between Financial Buyers and Strategic Buyers in a later chapter. The business owner had been shafted by the accountant he had trusted for many years. As time went by, he started to lose hope of ever selling his business. Eventually he did manage to sell his business a few years later but the business had contracted over time, and the profits dipped almost to the point of becoming a distressed business.

Quite often the owner of the small business has spent their whole lives running and growing their businesses. However, the expertise they have developed in their fields can blind them to the fact that they are not experts in what, for most, is the biggest and most important transaction of their professional lives; selling their business.

The second important aspect to bear in mind when considering the sale of your business, or part of it, is that it is a deeply emotional experience. We often like to think of business in terms of hard numbers and tough decisions. Selling your business, of course, also involves these elements. But for many, the most important element is the emotional one. You are setting a price and parting with something you have spent years of painstaking work creating, your baby. Your business has probably been the centre of your life for a long, long time. Many owners do not know how to deal with the rollercoaster of emotions that come with selling. Many of the staff are more like friends and family. They shy away from thinking deeply about what they want and why they want it. They end up being reactive rather than proactive, missing opportunities or failing to control events to achieve the best outcome.

We have put our personal assets at risk, we have signed over our homes as collateral for the much-needed bank loan, we have signed Personal Guarantees that we have never read, we have lost great employees and we have had employees steal from us.

We have had honest business partners and been betrayed by those we trusted. We borrowed money from friends, family and fools, we negotiated with business angels, venture capitalists and private equity investors, and battled with the banks. The last good fight is selling the business. We have to do this right; it is all that is left.

Chapter One: Are you ready to sell your business?

Selling a business has its ups and downs from start to finish and can be emotionally, physically and psychologically challenging. There will be challenges, surprises, disagreements and difficult questions to face. Buyers may have a very different perspective on your projections, the prospects of your market, the robustness of your intellectual property, your client list, your management and so on. Having the right advisor on your side, someone you like and trust who can anticipate and address these contingencies (and many more) is essential. This advisor must be able to build a positive rapport with each investor, be sensitive to the intricacies of the process, negotiate effectively and be someone you trust. He or she must have the right experience and be committed to your sales process. All of this will mean the highest likelihood of a successful outcome for you. Understanding the roles of the advisor will enable you to focus on the task in hand.

Lawyer

I was once asked to help sort out a Management Buyout for a £25m turnover construction company. The two owners had had a fallout and one of them, Ian, wanted to buy the other one, Andrew out. They had agreed a sum of £600k, that was cash in the business, but Andrew had been given some poor advice from his lawyer; that he would have to pay full tax of £240k on drawing out the £600k. Both party lawyers had been arguing, very slowly, back and forth for months with spiralling legal fees. I looked at the deal and suggested rather than Ian buyout Andrew, that the company buys back Andrew's shares and then he could qualify for Entrepreneurs Tax Relief and only pay £60k in tax. The lawyers didn't know what Share Buy Back was, as they were not M&A specialists or Tax Lawyers, just your regular high street business law fee earners. What should have been a very simple transaction that could have been resolved without Lawyers and using a Share Purchase Agreement ending up costing over **£50k in legal fees**.

Lawyers are not always necessary but if you do want to use them then you should negotiate a fixed fee. Another method which Lawyers don't like is that you as a seller can agree with the buyer on all the terms and then both of you go to a lawyer to draft the Share Purchase Agreement (for you both). Further in the book we discuss some of the elements that you can see in a Share Purchase Agreement. Our training course covers the Share Purchase Agreement in more detail so you will be equipped to handle a simple sale and purchase yourself and not need to pay such large legal fees.

Accountant

If you have an accountant that does your books, they might equally know of another entrepreneur who wants to buy a business and hence may be able to help you sell.

Ask them how many businesses they have sold and how they have created valuation they put on it... Accountancy is a broad topic, and no-one will be able to do everything. Creating the accounts is not the same as understanding providing business advice or creating a valuation.

Warning: An accountant told the entrepreneur that he could get a better price for his business than he was offered by an investor. The entrepreneur subsequently turned down the investor offer and trusted his accountant to get him a better deal. Eighteen months later the business had ceased trading and was being wound up.

The sales and marketing in selling your business, contrary to what you may think or what others may tell you, is not fundamentally a matter of accounting. While the numbers behind your business are important, it is primarily the effectiveness of the sales and marketing initiative that offers the highest probability of a successful transaction.

"What is my business worth?" is a legitimate question that most accountants are happy to answer immediately. You may hear some sort of rule of thumb like "6x-8x EBITDA is common in your industry", but always take such comments with the proverbial grain of salt. This is potentially wrong in your case and risks setting your expectations either too low or too high. Just ask the accountant how many companies he has sold in your industry. How is the accountant going to market your business for sale? I think you already know the answer to your questions and don't really need to ask.

What you can do is ask the accountant to put together your financials and forecasts with justifications on any increases. The accountant can also highlight any one-off expenditures that may have occurred in the last three years and adjust the profitability of the business accordingly. You do need to make sure that any adjustments are justified as stripping out expenditure which is essential to trading such as training courses will put off a buyer very quickly. You might want to highlight some add-backs too, these are items that may be accounted for in a different way in previous years to save you tax. One that you should understand is your role in the company; a prospective buyer may want to replace you with a salaried employee. A salaried employee to do your job may make £80k pa for example, but in your accounts, you are probably accounted for using the £12K tax allowance and the rest of your personal income is squirreled away in 'travel expenditure' and the likes. The rest of your income will be paid as dividends in a more tax efficient way. People who buy businesses are rarely looking to buy a job like yours. They are looking to create income streams.

You might also want your accountant to help in getting the business assets and stock valued. This isn't always the value currently depreciated on the balance sheet but will need a specialist valuation. If you have a lot of assets and stock you will probably need to seek the specialist help of a RICS valuer who is a specialist in your industry, don't rely on your Accountant to know everything.

Business Broker

Warning, this is an unregulated marketplace. We are not saying do not use a broker to sell your business but go in with your eyes wide open.

Reality check - Statistics show that 90% of businesses that are listed with business brokers DO NOT sell...

As most entrepreneurs have never sold a business you are yet to have the experience of dealing with a broker. Cast your mind back to the experience you had when selling your last home. They want your business, so sell you on the idea they have a boat load of buyers just waiting to snap up your property. They give you a slightly higher price expectation than their competition to get the deal and ask you to sign a 12-week sole agency agreement. (WHY not 2 weeks considering they told you they have a list of buyers ready to move?!)

Let's look at the Broker's business model and how they are paid.

Brokers make and expect most of their money from upfront fees. Selling the business will net them more but they are happy to wait as they have a way of getting more cash out of you.

They will charge an upfront fee for creating a seller's pack and loading the details of your business to their website among others. The seller pack will include them taking your last set of accounts and adjusting the figures. The adjustments are supposed to remove one off business expenses and revenues that affected the business as well as removing the business owner expenses that were put through to save tax.

Now read the small print. You are looking for a tie-in, cancellation fee, and is their commission for selling the business based on their valuation fee or the actual amount you receive?

Some brokers will then charge a monthly marketing fee to keep advertising your business. For them there is no additional expense for them, but they enjoy the extra income.

Brokers sit there aggressively waiting for the phone to ring. I rang a broker the other day as they had a business for sale and whilst I was not interested in the business, the business premise was leased and the perfect location for my son's new business venture. The broker admitted they did not do any outbound marketing to push the business and when challenged why it had not sold said, "it's only been on the market for 142 days". Needless to say, the business owner has yet to tie up a sale.

Even if a broker does manage to pick up the phone to a potential buyer, they do not understand some of the possible deal structures and do not want the prospective buyer to deal with the seller.

From our experience more often than not brokers negatively impact more deals than they tie up.

ONE OF THE REASONS I DO NOT USE BROKERS:

Here is a real-life example of the lengths a broker will go to when creating the adjusted accounts and valuation. For comparison purposes here are the original accounts filed at companies' house and the accounts produced by a prominent well-known business broker.

Year End:	31-Mar		
Year	2016	2017	2018
Fixed Assets			
Plant and machinery	£35,447	£26,585	£19,939
Office furniture & equipment	£1,276	£1,021	£817
Computer equipment	£6,368	£4,488	£7,908
Motor vehicles	£44,006	£43,014	£32,261
Sub-total	*£87,097*	*£75,108*	*£60,925*
Current Assets			
Stock	£52,000	£31,000	£40,500
Trade debtors	£366,369	£191,310	£206,198
Other debtors	£19,158	£19,687	£13,680
Amounts recoverable on contract	£0	£0	£0
VAT recoverable	£339	£862	£0
Cash at bank and in hand	£544,196	£463,983	£347,984
Sub-total	*£982,062*	*£706,842*	*£608,362*
Creditors: amounts falling due within one year			
Hire purchase contracts	£0	£0	£0
Trade creditors	£332,041	£238,169	£135,570
Taxation and social security	£31,419	£14,218	£19,403
Corporation tax	£63,144	£49,914	£39,575
Directors loan account	£63,937	£23,862	£39,900
Other creditors	£210,278	£25,980	£13,677
Sub-total	*£700,819*	*£352,143*	*£248,125*
Net current Assets	**£281,243**	**£354,699**	**£360,237**
Total assets less current liabilities	**£368,340**	**£429,807**	**£421,162**
Creditors: amounts falling due after more than one year			
Hire purchase contracts	£0	£0	£0
Sub-total	*£0*	*£0*	*£0*
Provisions for liabilities			
Deferred tax	£10,353	£8,282	£6,066
Total assets less liabilities	**£357,987**	**£421,525**	**£415,096**
Capital and reserves			
Called-up share capital	£102	£102	£100
Other reserves	£0	£0	£0
Retained earnings	£357,885	£421,423	£414,996
Shareholders' funds	**£357,987**	**£421,525**	**£415,096**

BALANCE SHEET
AS AT 31 OCTOBER 2018

Notes		2018 £
	CURRENT ASSETS	
3	Debtors	11135
	Cash at bank and in hand	18980
		30115
4	**CREDITORS** - amounts falling due within on year	(4412)
	NET ASSETS	**25703**
	CAPITAL AND RESERVES	
	Called-up share capital	2
	Profit and loss account	25701
	SHAREHOLDERS' FUNDS	**25703**

Yes, it is the same company. I did a double take when I saw this and then checked again.

Brokers frequently have adjusted profits in their Information Memorandum documents, such as the owner/director income as they are selling and leaving. This adds difficulty to negotiating after the broker has set expectations on high multiples of overinflated profits.

The main reason I don't use brokers and only use letters or referred opportunities is because 100% of my experience of dealing with a broker is they stop me getting the company.

Broker business model

Link to Jonathan Jay mystery shopper talking to the business broker trying to sell his business

https://www.youtube.com/watch?v=2hBaEpDdNII&ab_channel=JonathanJay

Summary paragraph

Not all brokers are the same. Smaller brokers tend to be better, but a final word of caution– Watch the fees and tie-ins!

There was another business broker story. When asked how he came up with the value for the business he answered that he simply took the number of shareholders and multiplied by £1m. Why? Because if you ask the majority of business owners what they want for the business you will get the answer, "One Million".

You have other options, otherwise you would not be reading this book.

Chapter Two: The emotions of selling

Entrepreneurs spend their lives running and growing their businesses. However, the expertise they've developed in their field can blind them to the fact that they aren't experts when it comes to the biggest and most important transaction of their professional lives, selling their business.

Selling is a process filled with emotions. Think about the last item you bought, think about how you 'felt'. Was it a decision from the head or the heart?

Today we are bombarded with so much advertising tugging on our emotions, making us feel good. If you are prone to impulse buying you will already have heard the best way to get over that is to take your credit card, put it in a freezer proof container, fill it with water and your card, pop it in the freezer and then go shopping. Now, when you see that next impulse buy you can't buy it. You rush home to try and free your credit card from its encasement in ice. By the time you get back to the store, guess what, the emotion has gone. You have had a chance to think with your head, "why am I buying it"? What benefit will it give me? You are questioning your motives and then going on to make an informed, balanced decision. And if you proceed with the purchase, it is for the right reasons.

The buyer of your business will be looking to buy your business for their own unique set of reasons. They do not have the emotional investment you have in the business. This is not a distance selling transaction with a fourteen-day cooling off period. When the deal closes that is it, you have sold your business.

One of the most important aspects to bear in mind when considering the sale of your business, or part of it, is that it's a deeply emotional experience. Often, when we think of business, we only think of hard numbers and tough decisions. Of course, selling your business involves these elements as well. But for many, the most important element is the emotional one. You're setting a price and parting with something you've worked hard to create over many years. Your business has probably been the centre of your life for a long time. The chances are that you have built your business from scratch. Some of the people you work with have crossed the boundary from just employees to friends and you might have members of your immediate or extended family working for/with you. Many owners don't know how to deal with the emotional rollercoaster that comes with selling.

There was one business we were looking to buy. Whilst there were 4 shareholders and directors, it was basically one person with the other 3 there by proxy. Any decision could be made by one brother, but the other brother and their wives were equally affected. The other brother and the niece wanted to stay on.

Because of the close relationship between the business owner and other team members, there are extra pressures and considerations a business owner will want to make. It is your business at the end of the day, and you have to do what is right for you, but by human nature you will want your "baby" to carry on and grow; to provide a safe and reliable haven for your staff, friends and family.

I spoke to the owner of one business. It was on spec and we had a great chat about his career and how he had grown the business, moved away and after a few years had bought back in. His son in law was probably the right person to hand over the reins to but there was some family friction at the time. Emotions were running high and with regards to making a balanced decision, then was not the right time.

As if you do not have enough to think about each day, you need to think about what you want, what your co-workers might want and then pitch your business to an interested party.

The trick to pitching your business is showing you are passionate about it; easy since you have lived and breathed it for years, but then making sure it fits with the buyer.

What you need to do is spend time with the buyer and understand their interest and motivations to look at your business. Having that insight and knowledge you can start to build the rapport that will allow you to really focus on showing the value in your business that meets and exceeds their needs.

You need to set your own expectations too. Some business owners get so wrapped up in the day to day running of their business that they fail to see the wood for the trees and realistically assess where the business is going and what it is worth. Some serial entrepreneurs will mentally check out of the business in favour of the next shiny opportunity and sell the business short of its value because they want to move on, and the marketing and sale of the business is taking too long.

Set yourself up with the right emotional mindset. Remind yourself of what you want and why you want it. That way you are being proactive rather than reactive. Your sole goal is to find the right opportunities and then control the events to help you achieve your best possible exit price and hopefully have some influence over the future of the team and business you will be leaving behind.

Chapter Three: Entrepreneurs are cut from a different cloth

We've put our personal wealth at risk, we've signed our houses as collateral for the much-needed bank loan, we've been stolen from by employees, and we've had employees stolen from us by competitors. We have had honest business partners and we were cheated by those we trusted. We borrowed money from friends, relatives and fools. We negotiated with venture capitalists and private equity investors; and we received numerous rejections before we got the long-awaited "yes" from the investor who finally got excited about our vision.

Mark's Story

Last century, I was working for EDS the large IT outsourcer that was purchased by HP Enterprise. I started working there whilst undertaking a Computing BSc degree at De Montfort University. Initially I was working in pre-sales, designing massive technical hardware infrastructure, technical configurations and design architecture for outsource deals for companies like Royals Royce (not the car company), Kellogg, BP, British Airways, London Marathon, Vickers (also not the car company but fasteners), Vickers (the car company), and many more major enterprises. The budgets for IT hardware and Software configurations were so large that if I wrote them here you wouldn't believe it. I was already entrepreneurial in ideas, and solutions to problems and was lucky enough to have quite a free reign in coming up with ideas that would transform businesses. This led to some interesting projects within EDS that included working with the management consultancy AT Kearney in Paris and building a 500-seat technical help desk in Peterlee County Durham; with the idea that not only would it consolidate 36 UK helpdesks but would lead on to mega global consolidated help desks around the world with a 24 hr follow the sun coverage. Alas, I never got to see my dream come true as I left on December 31st 1999 after being asked to run the Millennium Bug support desk on a 24hr shift after having my pay increase frozen and taken away after creating tens of millions of extra profits for EDS.

Following a brief spell at Royal Sun Alliance, Siemens Business Services and as the Senior International Consultant for an Enterprise Application Integration company called CommerceQuest, I decided to go it alone and setup a Purchasing Outsourcing company. It was there that I first met my long-term business partner in our IT company. We decided to merge and raised start-up finance. Then, just as the funds came in and business opportunities started flowing…

On 13th November 2003 I had a horrific car accident which saw the car barrel roll, flip head over heels, smash into a tree and explode in a ball of flames landing upside down with me still in it! I was able to get himself out of the car whilst on fire and put myself out before going looking for help. I had rolled the fire out on the grass verge, and my precious Ralph Lauren leather coat that I bought in New York, jeans and cotton shirt saved my life. I staggered down the road about 100 meters to the first house. Breathing was very difficult, and damage to my head meant my head was swelling and the vision had become tunnelled. I knocked on the first door, but as it was after midnight there was no answer, and the house was dark. With the damage to my lungs, I couldn't call out, so I headed to the next house. Just as I got to the next house and knocked, a lorry drove past. The lorry driver had called the emergency services. I was later told he had said no one could have survived this and when he saw the state of me, he himself was traumatised. I've always wanted to thank him and I'm sure he would want to know that I survived but data protection doesn't allow for me to get his details.

I actually sat down on the kerbside whilst waiting for the ambulance and had a cigarette, my last cigarette. I always joke to people, that I left my lighter in the car and had to use my hand to light the cigarette. One of my surgeons has often told that story to others, he himself can't believe I did that. That was the last time I smoked, when the fireman put me out.

At least I quit smoking, not the easiest way to quit and I wouldn't recommend this way to stop smoking.

I died twice over the next 48 hours and ended up in a coma, not waking up until a few days before Christmas. In the first 48 hours I spent the whole time in surgery having my hands rebuilt and skin grafts from all over, with burns to my head, torso, arms, hands, and leg. The prognosis was I was not going to live the next 24 hours. But I was stubborn and refused to give up.

When I first woke up, I was in a special heated room in the High Dependency Unit at Stoke Mandeville, the nurses worked a 12-hour shift in my room and then had to have two days off work. The room had special beds and I was fed through tubes directly to the stomach. I was bandaged from head to toe and there was no way to tell who was under there. I was on 100% respirator after both my lungs had failed, my kidneys had failed, my spleen and my pancreas had all failed and was kept alive by machines. I lost nearly 20 kilos in weight and was close to being a 6-foot skeleton at 50kg. I lost nearly all my muscle mass and needed to learn to walk again. Not just muscle wastage was an issue, after nearly two months in bandages over my eyes my vision had also disappeared. Even though I was told I wouldn't be out of hospital until March/April, I pushed himself through physio learning to walk again and was discharged on the 31st of December. I had sustained 64% burns to my body through the rule of nines measurement, and needed follow-up reconstructive surgery to my neck, face, mouth, and hands.

In January I went back to work, I had to, I had a new business and a young family to look after. If this was a situation where I was employed, I probably would have stayed in hospital and stayed off work for years. The next 15 years saw major reconstructive surgery nearly every year, it was a life of, surgery, recover and then back into surgery. I've had so many experimental procedures done, or first to have done in the UK, over the years and every type of skin graft including artificial dermis.

Being an entrepreneur with business commitments often meant when I woke up from the general anaesthetic I was immediately on the phone and laptop working. The 15 years following the accident I had spent over two years in hospital, all the time, taking care of my family and running the business. Driven, driven to succeed.

Business owners are driven to succeed. They are looking after their baby, and they will do whatever is needed to make shit happen; although on a few occasions I have seen business owners cross the line. Another merger that we undertook should have seen the business grow to more than double its size, but this new business partner wasn't as strait-laced as my current business partner. In fact, this new business partner turned out to be crooked and nearly cost us everything.

A merger that went wrong

Mergers are a great way to grow a business and improve profits. We quite often see industry consolidation bringing in big gains and strategic mergers even greater opportunities. Mergers can also be used as an exit where you hand over your key working role to the other party, take a lower salary but benefit from greater dividend pay-outs. In this example, before I knew how to make sure a merger works, I found out it can go wrong and this one went horribly wrong. In the end this merger only delivered a valuable life lesson and many, many lessons in business and mergers and insolvency.

One day I was at an event in Reading at Microsoft HQ when I bumped into an old friend who used to work for IBM. He used to sell into EDS PC's, Laptops and Servers, in particular he was the sales rep on a deal with British Airways Engineering. A complex deal where EDS were taking over the ownership of the assets and software. It was about 3000 PC's and 500 impact printers from Lexmark that needed to be in a cage and bolted down to the tables. Believe it or not, even with airside security being really tight, things had a habit of disappearing.

A funny side story on this particular deal, I was listening to a story from an engineer at CommerceQuest a few years later, who was running a project for Network Rail as a contractor. He had allocated 2500 PC's at the distributor and was waiting for sign off from the executives in Network Rail to buy the PC's. Eventually he got the approval and went to buy them, but they had all gone. It turned out that I was the person who had bought the whole supply chain of the PC's. He was actually fired from that role after missing the roll out deadlines and having the installation engineers all hired with nothing to do. Oops! Small world...Anyhow... back to IBM and British Airways Engineering.

The deal at EDS was very close to being rejected by the value review board at EDS as the breakeven point was going to be something like three years when the maximum is normally eighteen months. I had to spend about £5,000,000 on IT PC equipment on a deal where the margins were quite tight. I came up with the idea of putting all the equipment on finance, but EDS never approved finance as they didn't like paying the interest. So, I got the IBM sales rep to speak to IBM Finance and we managed to get a deal on 0% finance agreed about 10 minutes before the EDS Value Review Board sat down to discuss the deal and give it a green light.

This IBM Sales Rep, Brian, was someone that I had done deals with, sat with in hotel bars at Heathrow until the early hours of the morning, and became slightly more than just work acquaintances with. I actually brought him in to CommerceQuest as one of the initial Sales Reps and we flew all over Europe pitching Enterprise Application Integration deals to many B2B internet companies. After a couple of years at

CommerceQuest the internet bubble burst and everyone was laid off.

So, when we bumped into each other at Microsoft we sat down and had a chat. It turned out that he had started a B2B PC business in the south of England offering hardware sales and support. As I had a business in Milton Keynes also doing B2B IT Support, hardware sales, Internet connectivity, Mobile and fixed line telephones we discussed a merger. Even though his business turnover was only about a third of ours, he had plenty of customers that we could cross sell our other services into. We agreed a three-way split between myself my business partner, Dave, and the incoming friend from IBM, Brian. We issued shares and got about merging and selling of the services. A few months into this new merger and Brian disappeared. We had an agreement that we would take £3k per month against our directors' loan accounts to offset against dividends at the end of the year. Brian still took £3000 in September but nothing work-related, not a call or an email. Eventually he called and said he had an accident falling off a horse box and broke his arm and couldn't work.

Then there was the next reason Brian couldn't work; his father passed, and he was the executor of the estate, so he needed another couple of months off. A few months passed and eventually in January the three of us sat down and put together a sales strategy for the upcoming year.

Everything was going well. We had some nice large orders coming in and then in April Brian disappeared again. Dave tried calling Brian a number of times but no response, except for once when Brian picked up by accident and just stayed silent on the phone. Dave then got a call from Brian's girlfriend who was a nurse, who said Brian was ill and taking Desmopressin and was having side effects. I knew the name of the medicine from somewhere but couldn't remember where. Then a few days later I opened my medicine cupboard and there was a bottle subscribed for one of my young kids to help suppress bed wetting. In his witness statements, Brian wrote he was diagnosed with a suspected peptic ulcer, not sure how you can be diagnosed with a suspected ulcer, it's either diagnosed or it is not diagnosed. Why would you need anti bed wetting pills for an ulcer?

Next thing we heard from Brian was an Email in May saying he had taken £9,000 out as an advance of his £3,000 per month to pay for his honeymoon and he was getting married. Still no work from Brian or any form of contribution to the business. Then in June Brian took out another £3,000 with a message saying he needed it for a pre-honeymoon.

Enough was enough, Dave and I spoke to a lawyer, it was tough to do anything because we didn't have any agreements, no employment contracts for the three of us, no shareholder agreements, nothing. The lawyer said the best we could do was suspend Brian for Gross misconduct pending a hearing on the Monday after he got back from his honeymoon. We also contacted the bank and removed Brian from the account mandates so he couldn't take any more money for a post-honeymoon!

On the Saturday, on getting back from his honeymoon(s), Brian called Dave, ranting saying he would be in the office on Monday with his lawyer.

That Monday Dave waited in the office for the 10am meeting, he waited, and waited. Brian didn't show. What we did find out later that day was the bank account had been emptied. The next day we discovered from Barclays that Brian had forged paperwork showing he owned 100% of the business and Barclays gave him access without checking with the mandate holders, Dave and I.

What should have been a great merger, turnout to be a nightmare.

At first Brian continued down the route that he was 100% owner. He had been in the office at some point, probably the weekend he was back, and removed the folder with all the company documents and all the evidence. Luckily, I keep all my emails, millions of them, and I found evidence of the division of the shares. Brian continued down that route for a little while that he was 100% shareholder until we found out his lawyer stopped representing him. Then a few months later Brian resurfaced, this time with a new law firm paid via his home insurance and a new angle. Brian was now claiming he was just an employee, and we were satanic evil bosses. This new case dragged on and on.

We had a first hearing but in that hearing Brian declared that we had hacked his email, so it was suspended whilst the latest fabricated stories were investigated, this time by the Police. Once they were dismissed, we had to wait again. All in all, the legal cases took nearly two years. That is two years of trying to put together enough evidence to disprove lies. It is easy to prove the truth, not so easy to disprove lies from a serial cheater.

We actually discovered on this journey that Brian had also swindled his own brother out of his father's inheritance!

When the second hearing happened, we spent a few days in court before on the final day Brian agreed to a deal. He wanted £30,000 for his shares and agreed to being paid in instalments. The agreement was that for each £10,000 paid he would transfer a third of his shares across. We had to pay in instalments, at that time the legal fees had nearly wiped us out. There was also the two years we had spent with constant legal requirements meant the business was neglected and had suffered.

The first £10,000 had been paid and we requested the shares to be transferred, nothing, no response from Brian from our contact or his lawyers. We were most of the way through to the next £10,000 and there was still nothing. Our biggest issue was that like most directors we are paid in dividends. We couldn't award dividends as Brian was still technically a shareholder. So, we took some advice from a local Insolvency Practitioner who told us to close the old company and open a new one to remove Brian as the shareholder.

That turned out to be bad advice. Brian suddenly reappeared and objected to the winding up and a different Insolvency Practitioner was appointed who was very aggressive. They want all the directors loan accounts repaid which totalled approximately £150,000. They eventually accepted a payment plan but that meant we had to repay everything we were paid for the last two years.

This whole episode cost in the region of £250,000, not just because Brian was a crook, but more because we didn't do the deal properly and protect ourselves. A very expensive lesson learnt.

A merger is a very powerful way to grow the business and also a good way to exit the business as long as you do it right. I learnt the hard way how not to do a merger. I then studied how to do a merger, a sale and a purchase correctly and I'm very, very, proficient in the insolvency process too.

There's also when is the best time to sell, now…

This is a story from a good friend of mine who had the opportunity to sell his business but decided to keep going. It's a story of Jeremy not selling his call centre:

"Pretty much every reason you can think of for not selling your business is probably the reason for selling your business.

Many Moons ago, Jeremy owned two companies at the same time. One was a call centre business that was incredibly profitable. They had a three-year contract with the world's largest insurance company, and they were making £200,000 per quarter in net cash. It was a really great business. Jeremy had another business in the telecom space, which was doing okay but wasn't really increasing shareholder value year-on-year. His conventional thinking at the time was to sell the telecoms company, which was limping along and to keep the cash cow business, splitting off all the cash.

He went through the sales process on the telecoms company, which took a while and by the time I had sold it the call centre company had gone bust... the world's largest insurance company was called AIG. He had lots of problems with them, as he is sure lots of other companies did too.

His reason for not selling was that he had a 3-year contract with the world's largest insurance company

His reason for selling should have been because he had a 3-year contract with the world's largest insurance company.

If you are a business owner and you're thinking next year is going to be your best year ever, then sell it now. If next year is going to be your best year ever, the buyer is going to love your business. De-risk the deal and sell the business at what it's worth today, with an earn out linked to performance next year. So, when it doesn't actually do what you expect it to do because, 'hey this is business and when has it ever done exactly what you expect it to do?' you get the upside if it succeeds, and you do not have the risk of the downside if it fails."

PART II: How Much is My Life's Work Worth?

The truth is that the answer to this question depends on many factors, some of which you can control and some of which you cannot. Here is the very important point to remember when thinking about selling price: Your business will be sold at exactly the price someone is willing to pay for it.

Your business will sell at exactly the price someone is willing to pay for it.

Annually you ask your accountant to prepare the accounts so they can be filed with Companies House and HMRC. Most SME business owners will be looking for the accounts to reflect the most tax efficient picture possible. Makes sense as no-one enjoys paying tax and also it means you can keep more cash in the business for whatever value-added purpose you can envisage in the future. This may not lead to the best representation of the accounts from the perspective of achieving the best valuation for the business.

You are probably about to invest more time and effort in your business to come up with a valuation. You might be asking yourself why do that and why do that now?

Opportunities come along all the time, and you want to be ready to grasp them with both hands. By being prepared now means there will be less chance of you missing out on making the most of the opportunity. If someone was interested in buying your business tomorrow, where would you start in trying to sell the value that you have built up?

There are any number of reasons to want to understand the value of the business. More than one of the reasons on the list below might be on your mind for the near future:

- Time to sell or retire
- Merger or acquisition
- Buy out shareholder or Business Partner
- Want to invest more, good idea or poor return
- Time to IPO
- Want to raise finance or do a debt for equity swap

Are you adding value to the business? Are you spending your money on assets that are bringing a return or should you be selling / sweating your assets? If you have spare cash, do you look to buy back shares by buying out another shareholder or look to buy a supplier or a competitor? Maybe you want to take a dividend or maybe make an investment or if you cannot make a better return then maybe just go and buy a 911 (if only I had listened to my heart and bought that E-Type Jaguar when I was offered it. It would have been a better return on investment than my 911).

Note. A boat is not an investment, just a very expensive toy that will make you cry when you buy and cry when you sell.

The start point for any valuation is are you valuing the business as an ongoing concern?

For the non-accountants out there one of the 4 fundamental accounting principles is the Ongoing concern principle. The annual accounts are prepared based on values that would imply that the business will continue trading.

Okay so there may be no way to sell the business as an ongoing concern.

Reasons:

- You are the key person in the business. There is no business without you, the customers would leave, the suppliers would restrict the new owners or price them out.

- PEST issues – Political, Economic, Social and Technical factors have changed that now adversely affect the viability of the company

- The market has changed, too much competition or market trends have changed for the short or maybe even the long-term.

Not an attractive takeover target and you Can't find a buyer, so the only option is to wind down the business and rip out as much cash as possible as soon as possible.

At the end of the day this comes down to what you can get as a garage sale price

The £500k net book value of your plant and machinery is bespoke to your business, you might get 10-20% of what it is worth,

Stock – in your accounts is valued at the lower of cost and net realisable value. But what if you needed to sell or needed to sell quickly? Then you will only see a fraction of that value.

Sorry to hit you with this but there is no simple, single one size fits all route to a business valuation.

Hence the number of books, courses and the countless valuation methods taught at the Harvard Business School.

Every business is different. Even two businesses in the same industry of the same size could have totally different valuations. Why is that?

How is the business funded?

There are two ways to fund a business Debt or Equity.

In the case of Equity, the Owners, Investors and retained earnings from previous years provide the funds for the business. They expect a return, and the return is typically in the form of dividends. (Some companies will issue free shares and others have a no dividend policy meaning if the value of the company goes up then the investor can then sell some of their shares to get back their investment and any capital growth.

Depending on the company, dividend policy depends on the level of cash that leaves the business for future investment to drive the business forward.

The alternative is Debt – loans, debentures, HP and Lease Purchases. These require interest payments to be made, (unless you find interest free money in which case keep it a secret or give me a call).

The way dividends and interest are booked in the accounts has an effect on a valuation.

How well run is the company? – Does it have a strong growing cashflow, over the last 5 years are there steady earnings or are they flat or growing?

What are the business risks? – Is it reliant on a small number of customers, is it a player in a niche sector and if so is it a small or a big fish in that pond?

What is the product mix?

Where in the market cycle or business cycle is it? Is it growing, a cash cow or declining?

So many questions all which have a bearing on a valuation.

Predictable earnings will usually imply a better multiple as less risk to an investor (investors hate unknowns or volatility)

Manufacturing v Service Industry?

Capital intensive v labour intensive business?

Start up or a mature business

We have all seen Dragons' Den and the over valuations and the higher percentage the Dragons want to mitigate risk, represent the time they need to spend and the estimated additional value they can bring. Valuation is even harder for businesses with no proven business model, proven track record, solid orders, low revenues and questionable profits and forecasts for the next 3-5 years.

PLC v LTD

There is plenty of information about a PLC, what it is doing, where it is going, regular statements, updates etc. and then there is all the financial information – accounts, bad debts, borrowing and Share price. Very easy to find the information and assess the value of the business and determine if the share price represents value for money.

Also look out for insiders (CEO, CFO etc.) trading their companies' shares.

There are plenty of books and sources that will explain about PE Ratios, EPS (Earnings per share) and Market capitalisation calculators, but that is not the focus of this book.

However, when it comes to the LTD there is little to no info, accounts can be filed 9 months after they close.... Anything can happen in that time.

Companies House will have some financials, but the filings requirements differ depending on company size.

Also, you could look at a comparable – companies' same industry and size – look at competitors. It will also allow you to decide if you are doing better than them and massage your ego. Failing that, you might be knocking spots off them and could be a takeover target or they might be your way to sell and move on / retire.

Chapter Four: Valuation

There are many different ways to come up with a value for the business, one Harvard Business School study found 126 ways that a business could be valued. You would need to attend a Harvard MBA course to understand them all, but in reality, for a small to medium business such as yours, a multiple of profits will be all that will be required as the most widely used valuation method. Although a multiple of profits is the most common valuation method used it could be that one of the other well-known methods of valuation could be appropriate. Quite often in a discussion on price, the price that can be justified and evidenced is the price a business sells for.

In one initial meeting with a scaffolding business the seller did not know how to sell a business or how to value the business. The seller had heard about multiples and a multiple of x3 as being an average, so the conversation was going well as that is around the average multiple for an SME Business. In this specific scenario there were actually two different companies up for sale, one was the sales and marketing side of the business and the second was more the operational side of the business that also included the assets in the business. The scaffolding had been written down by the accountant over three years when in reality the assets lasted well over ten years, but the value was not visible. There was also an issue between the two companies in the VAT intercompany billing, but we did not examine this in any detail but made a note to examine the VAT accounts and intercompany transfers as part of the financial due diligence. On touring the factory there was a vast amount of scaffolding and associated accessories so there was a lot of hidden value that was not discussed. It then came to talking turkey. The businesses had a combined turnover of about £3m and profits of about £250k but the owner had hidden some of his expenditure within business expenditure. On being asked what value he placed on the business he quoted "a multiple of three so £9m". He had already in his mind bought a Ferrari, land for a vineyard and a holiday. His dreams were then shattered when he discovered the multiples were on profits and not turnover. However, in his circumstances a multiple of profits may not have been the best method to value the business.

At the end of the day one valuation method will not fit all and yes, the basic is cash in – cash out = profit. For example, a local undertaker - a niche regulated stable business v a contractor recruitment / temp agency v a telecom company. They all have different business structures and requirements.

And add to that the fact businesses have different requirements and profiles depending how mature they are. For example, Telcom companies have high up-front investment costs and then only get paid a subscription monthly, so they have high asset and initial working capital requirements.

Accounts are put together using a predefined set of rules and the reporting requirements based on the size of the company are also defined. The smaller the business the less detail making getting the information that much harder.

Are the accounts audited? – This offers a more consistent approach as an external auditor has to sign off to the effect the accounts reflect a true and fair view of the business.

In the UK every company needs an audit. Don't panic there are exemptions. A small company is exempt from audit if over the current and previous year two of the following thresholds were not breached.

1. Turnover >= £10.2m
2. Balance sheet >= £5.1m
3. Number of Employees >= 50 employees

Even if your company is usually exempt from an audit, you must get your accounts audited if shareholders who own at least

10% of shares (by number or value) ask you to. This can either be an individual shareholder or a group of shareholders.

Can I or should I be making any adjustments to the accounts?

The simple answer is yes, but you must justify the adjustments and detail what they are for. I have seen Brokers try to adjust the accounts for business expense for staff training in a gas boiler business which was essential and a legal requirement. When it is for personal expenditure that is not part of the day-to-day operations, you should remove them from the business expense and improve your profitability, especially when using a profit multiplier for the valuation.

In the USA a corporation doesn't use a P&L and rarely even a cashflow. Their annual accounts take the form of a tax return, and many things can be hidden in business expenditure. One security company was installing security cameras, building access, and proving the monitoring services for the cameras and door entry throughout Florida. As there were no cashflows or P&L the deal team decide to create one from the bank statements using our templates:

https://www.GoSellMyBusiness.com/CashFlow

After examining the bank statement, we found a number of anomalies and had a call with the seller to ask questions. Several of the entries were lifestyle expenses like going out to Hooters for dinner, getting a haircut, trips to the racetrack but the one item that just could not have been a legitimate business expense was when he went to swimwear and lingerie shop for his 'Wife and His Girlfriend'.

LIFE STYLE BUSINESSES HAVE LIFESTYLE EXPENSE

5/4/18	Point Of Sale Withdrawal HOOTERS PALM BAY PALM BAY FLUS		-40.89	45,305.96
5/4/18	External Deposit INTUIT PYMT SOLN - DEPOSIT 524771998014622	2,903.94		48,209.90
5/4/18	External Withdrawal INTUIT PYMT SOLN - TRAN FEE 524771998014622		-80.14	48,129.76
5/5/18	Point Of Sale Withdrawal LONGHORN 00054MELBOURNE FLUS		-42.15	48,087.61
5/5/18	Point Of Sale Withdrawal SQ *ALFIE'S BARBER Melbourne FLUS		-65.00	48,022.61
5/5/18	Point Of Sale Withdrawal WAGON WHEEL PIZZA MELBOURNE FLUS		-31.17	47,991.44
5/6/18	Point Of Sale Withdrawal WASTE MGMT WM EZPAY866-834-2080 TXUS		-30.57	47,960.87
5/6/18	Point Of Sale Withdrawal APL* ITUNES.COM/BIL866-712-7753 CAUS		-29.99	47,930.88
5/7/18	Point Of Sale Withdrawal PANE E VINO ITALIANMELBOURNE FLUS		-108.92	47,821.96
5/7/18	External Withdrawal IRS - USATAXPYMT 227852766008882		-1223.61	46,598.35
5/7/18	Point Of Sale Withdrawal RACETRAC 2396 745 PALM BAY RD WEST MELBOURN FLUS		-72.50	46,525.85

One time / exceptional revenues and expenses. These are not typical cash flows and are not expected to occur again, so they can legitimately be removed to more accurately reflect the true business performance.

e.g., Cost of closing a business or laying off staff or a profit / loss on the sale of a fixed asset, Cost of an IT refresh after being hacked...

Offloading or closing down part of the business is another legitimate adjustment. Simply split the revenues and costs to allow the true ongoing business activities and trends to be visible. PLC's have a requirement in their financial statements to report any discontinued activities.

E.g., discontinued product (trends change / superseded / overtaken by competitor and retired from the sector), change in go to market channels (direct v indirect/partners), change in Geography (e.g., opening a new market)

Personal / owner expenses - these should be identifiable; the new owners will have their own idea as to what they want to get out of and put through the business and need to understand what you do.

E.g., we have seen business brokers rip out so much as part of restating accounts and then have the audacity to say the loss-making business is profitable – yes as the new business owner you might be happy earning £5000 per year....

Discretionary expenses

These are the expenses that you should be reviewing annually to ensure not wasting cash.

For example, is a water cooler the best option? When did you last change or review utility and insurance suppliers, accountants etc? If you have not genuinely reviewed and amended, then you should not be amending them now.

Charitable donations are commendable but would typically be removed.

You can guarantee that any prospective buyer of the business will be looking for potential savings. They will look for any number of opportunities to restructure, cut costs, sweat the assets, divest or diversify, merge and employ a number of financial improvement / re-engineering techniques. So, allocate some time now, whilst thinking about a possible sale, to improving the financial position. After all, you want to be able to achieve the best possible valuation for you.

Imagine you have bought that boat.

- A sailing boat needs to be trimmed and the sails tight to get the best performance.

- You need to service your motorboat annually and have the antifouling done to ensure maximum speed and fuel efficiency as you power through the water.

Caveat – at the end of the day you can hide or amend all you like. The new owner / investors will find out the real state of affairs anyway. They will protect themselves and will be doing their own due diligence, so any adjustments you make may as well be open and transparent.

Contracts.

Do you have contracts in place? Probably yes from a supplier perspective. A prospective buyer will want to look at these for length, tie-ins and rate rises, and they will determine if the contracts secure a beneficial interest to supply and future cash flow.

Now, do you have contracts in place with any customers? Having a contract in place helps guarantee the reliability of the future cash flows and hence adds value to a business and can help reduce the risk profile for the prospective buyer.

A new investor will also be looking for areas of improvement, after all the new owners will be buying in to make a return on their investment.

We cover the four most commonly used valuation methods in this book

- Multiple of Profits
- Discounted Cash Flow
- Revenue Multiple Method
- Book Value / Asset Value Multiple

and we discuss another valuation method on the course we run.

Multiple of Profits

This method relies on EBITDA. For those non accountants if you substitute Net Profit for EBITDA, you will be closed enough

EBITDA – Earnings, before Interest, Tax, Depreciation and Amortization

Or to coin a phrase that I heard in the case of the financial scandal at US Telco – 'Earnings Before I Tricked De Auditors'.

Commonly used as a valuation method, it is simple to calculate but should not be used exclusively on its own.

EBITDA shows the net operating income which allows an investor to look at the operational effectiveness of a business. It removes the impact of interest charges which fund the financing of the business and by removing depreciation, as this removes the effect of a high value of asset in a business or where there has been a significant investment in new assets which will be used to drive future revenue and profits.

This method works for any size of business, from a small private business up to the large publicly listed companies. This is because once you have stripped away the tax and financing you can compare similar companies to gauge which is run better.

Remember you might be the perfect takeover target by one of your competitors... Or you could buy them if you see an opportunity to run it better.

<u>How to Calculate</u>

The more data you have the better, so ideally get hold of five years of accounts. Use three as a minimum. Both rely on the assumption future figures continue in a similar trend as the previous years.

We don't want to get too mathematical but note that if in one year there was a LOSS the formula does not work, and you will need to use future predictions on top of the actual profitable years.

When this method is applied to small businesses the challenge will always be trying to get the detail from the business owner's accounts.

The downside is that it does not relate to cash, so an investor needs to understand the difference between profit and cash.

Having got the EDITDA figure you need to look up and apply the relative multiplier to come up with the valuation.

Here is a look up table with historic as well as the latest annually published rates by sector:

https://www.GoSellMyBusiness.com/ProfitMultipleReports

This method relies on earnings and their predictability, but it could be used for start-ups but will require your best predictions hat and apply a risk factor to that calculation

Profit Multiple Method

Multiple	2.9						
			Actual Figures		Forecast Figures		
Fiscal Year		2020	2021	2022	2023	2024	Total
EBITDA		1,143,450	1,194,270	1,168,860	1,232,385	1,245,090	5,984,055
Weighting		1	2	3	4	5	15
Weighted EBITDA		1,143,450	2,388,540	3,506,580	4,929,540	6,225,450	18,193,560
						Average EBITDA	1,212,904
						Multiple	2.9
Valuation		**EBITDA X Multiple**					**3,517,422**

Note: Whilst EBITDA is better, taking the Net Profit figure will be useful if you can not define the EBITDA

Discounted Cash Flow

As valuation methods go this is as much an art as a science when it comes to calculating the value of a business. It is generally based on rigorous academic theory and can be used to establish a realistic range of valuation.

This is more for the mathematically minded. It is all about creating a forecast for the next few years and the applying an investor's expected return to determine what the future net cash flow is worth in today.

Whilst there is a scientific way to calculate a definitive value, it does call for some artistic license or phrased differently, careful consideration around the assumptions you make regarding the revenues and costs that influence the future cash flows and the discount rate to be used.

https://www.GoSellMyBusiness.com/Valuation

So, how far should you try and forecast and what assumptions would be reasonable? Realistically a buyer and a seller will have different thoughts on any assumption.

This Method assumes you can accurately PREDICT the future! And when modelling, the assumption you should make is HOW you would run the company in the future and model based on that. Some of the financial engineering techniques we use to turnaround distressed businesses can be applied to profitable businesses to increase the profits and hence the future value of the business.

How to Calculate

In reality, budgeting for the next 5 years is as far as you want to go as the assumptions start to get a bit vague, so do not try and over engineer this.

This calculation starts with free cash flow (FCF), which is roughly calculated as (net income + interest expense + depreciation) - (investments + changes in working capital) = FCF. "Investments" are expenditures on long-term assets; "working capital" would be, for example, investments in inventories.

Once you have calculated the free cash flow over time, a discount rate is applied. This rate is based on the risk of the cash flows. Once the FCF has been projected for a certain period of time (usually around five years), a terminal value is calculated, usually as a perpetuity (e.g. assuming that the company operates in perpetuity at a growth rate that correlates with GDP growth, e.g. 2% to 3%) or as a multiple of last year's EBITDA. Finally, a discount rate is applied to the projected cash flows to reduce the value of future cash flows by two factors; the time value of money (a dollar today is worth more than a dollar tomorrow) and risk (the projected dollar of EBITDA in the future might actually end up being 50 cents). Once these factors have been calculated, you can discount the projected cash flow to determine today's "valuation":

Discounted Cash Flow									
			ACTUAL				FORECAST		
Fiscal Year		2018	2019	2020	2021	2022	2023	2024	2025
Sales		£8,958,588	£8,900,000	£8,800,000	£8,727,608	£8,648,314	£8,569,020	£8,489,726	£8,410,432
EBITDA		£1,841,111	£1,800,000	£1,800,000	£1,772,593	£1,752,037	£1,731,482	£1,710,926	£1,690,371
		20.55%	20.22%	20.45%	20.31%	20.26%	20.21%	20.15%	20.10%
Post Tax Profit		£842,426	£800,000	£800,000	£771,716	£750,503	£729,290	£708,077	£686,864
		9.40%	8.99%	9.09%	8.84%	8.68%	8.51%	8.34%	8.17%
DCF					**£ 5,200,289**				
20%	**Investors expected return**								

Revenue Multiple Method

Where a company generates strong revenues with a minimal asset base to support the revenue then the better value is arrived at by using the Revenue Multiple method.

Companies and business owners often use this in addition to EBITDA, giving them a better view of not only the revenues but also how well run a business is.

This is a simple method to use and does not rely on the business being profitable and can be done as a quick and ready reckoner before spending too much time analysing a set of books.

Again, this valuation method predominantly relies on historical information. Even so, you need to consider the wider P.E.S.T. impacts on the future earnings and viability of the business and sector.

- Political: New regulations and trade restrictions may be on the horizon

- Economic: What is the impact of Interest rates, Inflation and a looming recession?

- Social: Generation X feel privileged and don't want to pick fruit for a living, electric cars need minimal maintenance so expect local garages to disappear

- Technical: Oil and Gas being phased out, improvements in battery technology will drive new electric vehicles (boats, cars and planes) ranges and abilities

<u>How to Calculate</u>

Using the Profit and Loss account figures take the Revenue Line for the last 5 years and calculate the average revenue per year. Now apply the relevant multiplier. This is different to the previous link to the Profit Multiple Reports. The Revenue Multiplier Reports

https://www.GoSellMyBusiness.com/RevenueMultiplierReports

Note the statistical multiples by industry that will give a value based on Revenue values and these are lower than the profit multipliers and range between 0.5 and 3.

Revenue Multiple Method							
Multiple	0.75						
			Actual Figures				
Fiscal Year	2018	2019	2020	2021	2022		Total
Revenue	4,500,000	4,700,000	4,600,000	4,850,000	4,900,000		23,550,000
Weighting	1	2	3	4	5		15
Weighted Revenue	4,500,000	9,400,000	13,800,000	19,400,000	24,500,000		71,600,000
					Average Revenue		4,773,333
					Multiple		0.75
Valuation	**Average Annual Revenue X Multiple**						**3,580,000**

Book Value / Asset Value Multiple

This is the least commonly used method as it really only applies to Capital Intensive companies. As the name suggests, this is due to the type of business and the equipment needed to run it to generate the revenues.

- Utility and Telecoms companies need to invest in the infrastructure to be able to supply the service

- The same applies to Car Manufacturing where huge upfront investment is needed in tooling and machinery. (Less of an issue for boat builders who just need a jig for the fiberglass hull and a hoist to help drop in the engines)

- Any company, whose business model relies on a property portfolio - (not ready for a Churchill retirement home yet)

- This method is also a viable valuation option for banks, financial institutions and Insurance companies

This method is great for identifying if a company is undervalued, and potentially an asset stripping target.

<u>How to Calculate</u>

Use the balance sheet and take the Total Value of the Shareholders equity and apply a multiplier. Multiples tend to be between 1 and 5 but you will need to look at some comparable companies in the same sector. Multiples for the Finance section tend to be lower at between 1 and 3.

Book Value / Asset Value Method						
Multiple	1.9					
				Actual Figures		
Fiscal Year		2018	2019	2020	2021	2022
Total Equity						1,850,000
					Multiple	1.9
Valuation		**Total Shareholder Equity X Multiple**				**3,515,000**

This method can be used by M&A Investors to find businesses that are valued at or near the book value. Wouldn't it be great to find a business to buy whose value is less than the actual costs of the assets? Perfect for asset stripping. I'm reminded of the line in Pretty Woman where Richard Gere's character said the second company that he bought was his father's and he sold it off piece by piece.

Distressed Liquidation Sale

Not every business is valued as a going concern. Where a business has got itself into trouble and has racked up debts then it is time to call in an Investor with turnaround experience, or an Insolvency Practitioner to restructure the business and the debt as a last-ditch attempt before throwing in the towel and winding up.

In this situation the SME business owner is probably in unchartered territory and is unaware of their options. They could also be staring down the barrel of a number of Personal Guarantees on loans that the creditor might be about to consider calling in.

Time is of the essence in these situations. In the unlikely event you are in that situation call us. I say that as it is unlikely you will be reading this book.

Overloaded? Keep it simple

Multiple valuation methods and theory is all well and good, but how do I as an SME business owner try and arrive at a valuation?

Well, try a few methods and see how the value differs. Then look at the reason for the difference and that will help guide you

One other question for you: Do you have a Lifestyle Business? A lifestyle business is designed around and funds the owner. Take the owner out and there is not much left. Also, an owner will take out the income they want; that may be the market rate, or it might be a gravy train until the day they want to bail.

Offers are rarely a suitcase full of cash or single bank transfer. An offer could be cash, deferred and earnout (that is a whole topic on its own), and the multiple might be higher to reflect a debt or long-term structured offer.

Company owners will often use multiple valuation methods to come up with a value. This will then give them an idea. Clearly an investor will do the same in reverse and there will be adjustments and negotiations to agree in the middle.

The next step…

Value your business NOW and periodically going forward.

Learn how to prep it for sale and learn the process in a safe supported environment.

Understand that the valuation does not mean a suitcase full of cash is usually on offer and everything is up for negotiating. It's a bit like buying a house (or a boat); it is only worth what someone is prepared to pay.

https://www.GoSellMyBusiness.com/Valuation

Chapter Five: Who will buy my business?

There are two types of buyers who will be interested in your business. One is a financial buyer who might not be from your industry and will treat the acquisition as an investment. The second is a more strategic buyer who is looking to add to their business or group. They each have a value model in what they will want to achieve their goals, and neither will treat the purchase of your business as a commodity or product purchase. It is seen purely as an investment and they will look at risk mitigation. Knowing who will be likely to buy your business is very important in understanding how to package and promote it. Understanding their motivations is where you need to be and knowing your motivations will help you create a win-win scenario. A financial buyer will be more interested in a profit multiple situation, whereas a strategic buyer maybe more interested in the assets that are in your business such as contracts and intellectual property. How a buyer will value your business and the methods they may use needs to be the strategy you adopt in promoting your business and packaging the marketing material in an Information Memorandum.

Different industries have different ways that they prefer to value a business. If you look at the acquisition of LinkedIn by Microsoft for $26 billion this had nothing to do with a P/E ratio but more to do with the 433 million customer acquisition. It was also the ability to embed LinkedIn into their other applications. This acquisition was also an entry into social media, but social media for business and the deep integration into the enterprise software of the Office 365 platform and the Dynamics CRM suit of apps. Microsoft, in this scenario, were using a price based on barriers to entry, as in what would it cost them to build the same and how long would it take?

Microsoft also bought Nokia for an entry in to the $50bn mobile market sector opportunity. A $7 billion acquisition seen as an opportunity to enter the mobile market to compete with Apple and Samsung. In a statement Microsoft says: "With a deeper understanding of hardware and software working as one, the company will strengthen and grow demand for Windows devices overall." However, step forward a few years and Microsoft had actually purchased a bit of an archaic dinosaur of a phone and struggled competing with Apple and Samsung, eventually pulling out of the mobile market altogether. In 2007 Microsoft Mobile OS had a market share of 42% of smart phone devices in the USA at its peak. By 2010 the US market share of the Microsoft Mobile OS had slipped to just 7% and just 3% when they acquired Nokia in 2013. Maybe if Microsoft had reacted in 2007 and become a hardware and Mobile OS company they could well have competed with Apple OS and Android.

Obviously, Microsoft purse strings are significant and in fact they don't really need to pay cash, they can pay by issuing shares. For example, let's say Microsoft was worth $1bn and had 1bn shares at $1 per share to keep it simple. Now if they go on a buying spree and purchase Minecraft and Activision creating $100m of additional value, this means that post deal valuation of Microsoft is now worth $1.1bn. So, they can issue 100m new shares without diluting shareholder value. The post deal valuation of Minecraft and Activision became a massive strategic bolt-on to the Microsoft gaming platforms, especially for the Xbox vastly increasing the value of Minecraft, Activision and Xbox. This type of acquisition is likely to create more value for Microsoft with the strategic nature of the deal. The value of Microsoft may well end up being a post deal valuation of $1.2bn, increasing shareholder value and increasing the share price. So, your $1 share has now grown in value to $1.1 dollar per share. Obviously, these calculations ignore the stock market hype where the share price may well have jumped to $1.5 per share just because of the high p/e ratio that a company like Microsoft commands.

Then we have Facebook who bought WhatsApp for $14 billion. This is a company that does not make any money and that's a massive p/e ratio, but Facebook didn't buy WhatsApp for the profits. They bought WhatsApp because they saw them not only as a competitor but as a threat and a Facebook Messenger killer. The strange thing was that WhatsApp wasn't really used that much in the USA, but it was used widely in the rest of the world and was rapidly gaining traction in the USA market. While Skype (owned by Microsoft and now part of their fully integrated enterprise messaging portfolio, Teams) was the biggest mobile messenger app in the US and Facebook second, WhatsApp had suddenly rocketed to the number 3 messenger app and was heavily out pacing Facebook Messenger. Nearly 10 years on since the purchase of WhatsApp and it is difficult to understand the commercials behind the acquisition except for it pushed the Facebook user base over the 1 billion user mark. The acquisition of Instagram who were bought for $1 billion by Facebook made more sense as just as Facebook is in the Advertisement Media space, so is Instagram. Instagram and Facebook have now become more closely integrated, helping Instagram's revenues and earning grow. Instagram has also benefited from using the Facebook infrastructure delivering scale and significant intrinsic value.

Ok, but your business probably won't be a target for Microsoft or Facebook, but similar strategies can exist in finding who will buy your business. So, who will?

Well, there are financial buyers (these are people who may have sold their business, reached a height within the sector that they are experts in your marketplace and have the ability to raise finance), serial entrepreneurs who acquire companies through debt, and if you are big enough private equity or venture capitalists. Finding these types of buyers can be quite difficult, which is one of the reasons we have developed our Buyers and Seller Dating App.

The next type of buyer is the strategic buyer. These are industry specific companies that may be suppliers, customers, competitors or a parallel sector wanting to break into your sector the same way that Microsoft wanted to break into the mobile marketplace.

Supply chain usually look to acquire their customers or suppliers in order to combine elements of the supply chain, similar to how Microsoft purchased Minecraft and Activision. By combining two parts of the supply chain, an acquirer may be able to achieve higher margins and gain access to a more attractive customer base. Both Sony with their PlayStation and Microsoft with their Xbox have done this to add new games, exclusive to their respective platforms, creating more demand to buy their console. Games like Halo, Assassins Creed, and Resident Evil have even crossed into the movie and TV entertainment division, with Lara Croft Tomb Raider generating over $275m global box office sales.

There are also competitors who may try to take over your business to consolidate their position in the market and gain more leverage in negotiations with suppliers and customers. You may have heard about fragmented sectors that are being consolidated. This happens frequently in the Telecoms sector when a small company is acquired by another larger telecoms company. Whilst writing this book I am involved in a similar play in the digital marketing sector where we are building a group of digital marketers to create a larger group. We are finding digital marketing companies in the £1-£5m turnover and creating a group. At launch we are expecting a group turnover of £20m with a goal to grow this to £50-£100m ready for a strategic exit. A smaller company may only have a profit multiple of circa 2.8x whereas a larger company may have a profit multiple of 8x/12x depending on the sector.

You may also find competitors in the same neighbourhood, by this I mean companies that are either in the same industry in a different region or sell a similar product to you in the same region. They may be wanting to acquire you to add to or strengthen a vertical within their own portfolio. A neighbouring product or services business may be wanting to add to their geography for example a US company buying a UK company to enter the region. What you may find is that strategic buyers are willing to pay a premium for your company, mainly because they don't actually want your company; they want what your baby has produced. This is one of the areas our consultants focus on in creating a better profit multiple for your exit with their global networks. This doesn't suit all businesses and it is best that you give us a call and have a chat about any possibilities that may exist for your business sector.

As a business gets bigger, so does the market of potential buyers up to a point – you can tip the scales and only have a few companies that are bigger than you, so your exit space gets smaller. For example, for a typical deal valued at £20 million or less, we have specialist advisors that build a list of suitors and engage with them on your behalf. We usually get an extensive list of potential strategic buyers compiled and market to them with great success. We also have a financial investor dating service where we match buyers and sellers together. It all starts with how you market your business and that needs to be constructed in a way that attracts your potential buyers. This is a specifically targeted brochure or in the investor's world an Information Memorandum, which will be discussed in more detail in the pre-marketing your business section.

Financial Buyers

A financial buyer is an investor who is interested in the income he can earn by buying a business. The financial buyer will not necessarily be looking for a job so when they look at your business, they will be looking to adjust the financials to accommodate replacing you or retaining you on a salary. They will keep track of the profitability of the company and the future exit opportunities the company is likely to offer. Financial buyers are opportunistic buyers who may or may not have expertise in your industry. The financial buyer should be seen very much as an investor who is gambling on creating more value over the next three to five years – when they will in turn look to exit.

A financial buyer may often take on significant debt to finance an acquisition, leveraging the company assets in a purchasing method referred to as Leveraged Buy Outs (LBO). They will look at the value of the fixed assets that can be refinanced to generate funds to buy the business. They will also look at the debtor book to raise finance against outstanding invoices. Additionally, they will look at any excess Cash at bank to fund the deal structure.

Also of importance for the financial buyer is the stability of the business. If the last five years books have any fluctuations, they will want to mitigate the risk in future trading. They will most definitely look at putting in deferred payments based on future performance. When you are selling your business, you will no doubt paint a rosy picture for the future. Or, if you have been to see a Broker, they will have elevated your growth to stupid levels. I have seen a business which had steady income for the previous five years and the Broker projects a 100% growth in turnover within two years. From an investor outside looking in it doesn't look realistic or even honest. An investor will quickly see through the smoke and mirrors of exaggerated forecasts and ridiculous adjustments to try and make the company seem more profitable. In the end all that happens is you will have lost an opportunity and paid the broker a lot of money in the process.

Financial buyers may also look to undertake a broader consolidation (buying and integrating companies in a particular sector to increase market power and achieve economies of scale). The marketing vertical that I am advising on is bringing together many companies together into a virtual consolidation play in the digital marketing sector.

They look for opportunities to invest in undervalued companies and/or companies poised for significant growth or market consolidation. During the period they hold the investment, they provide the necessary financial support for growth and plan to sell their investment at a profit in the short to medium term. Financial buyers primarily seek to profit by restructuring the operating and capital structure of your business – cutting costs, taking on more debt and using leverage – with the intention of selling their investment at a profit in the future. The usual holding period, for example, is five to seven years. Buying your company for a multiple of 2.9x (2021 average, or 2.7x 2018 average) means that for the next three years there may be nothing but paying down the Leverage Buy Out debt before they can realise any return on their purchase of your company. They will also look to mitigate the risk in change of ownership brings by putting in place earnouts and/or deferred consideration, or other similar risk mitigation strategies.

A financial investor's most desirable targets typically have reliable, established cash flows, high growth, low capital expenditure requirements, an established market position and products or services in growing markets and industries. However, different financial investors also use different investment strategies or they may be turnaround specialists who buy companies in trouble, make major changes to the company, negotiate with creditors and sell the company once it stabilises.

Financial buyers buy exactly what the company has to offer based on past performance and rarely on the company's expected future earnings at the time of the acquisition. They will rely on statistics of companies actually sold recently and the market multiples which average at a multiple of 2.9x adjusted profits and then they will adjust that multiple depending on factors such as current management.

https://www.GoSellMyBusiness.com/ProfitMultipleReports)

While they recognise the potential for cash flow expansion beyond what the company has achieved on its own, they are usually not willing to pay for that potential. Most financial buyers intend to grow the business and eventually sell it to a strategic buyer or, if necessary, take it public. An important distinction between the two main categories of investors, financial buyers and strategic buyers, is that the financial buyer often needs to be able to leverage the business, i.e. borrow money for their investment and pay the interest out of operating profits. The availability and cost of borrowed capital, among other considerations, can limit the price these investors are willing to pay. Financial buyers tend to be extremely sophisticated in terms of structure and due diligence. They usually have the in-house expertise to conduct in-depth analysis, model the value of potential acquisitions, structure the transaction and have the necessary legal expertise to get the deal over the line. Because they focus on debt service as part of the deal, issues such as quality, depth and experience of management, sustainable profits and free cash flow are topics to which the financial investor is more sensitive. There are advantages for financial buyers that if you know what they are looking for you can paint a much brighter picture for them and make it easier for them to buy your business.

There are a lot more financial buyers out there, but they can be harder to find. This is why entrepreneurs like yourself end up going with brokers as they pretend to have an unlimited number of people lining up with bags of cash to buy your company. We have setup a dating service with our extensive network of financial buyers which you can register for here: https://www.GoSellMyBusiness.com/FinancialBuyerNetwork

Another thing that will attract a Financial Buyer who may have a focus on future acquisitions and other growth initiatives is a list of companies like yours that they may want to go and target for acquisition and merger strategies. You can also list in your Information Memorandum and potential future performance improvement and growth opportunities, but don't build them into your forecast. You can quantify them in your Information Memorandum but just don't go down the route that brokers take and build them in to your sales price.

Typically, a financial buyer will have greater flexibility in determining the most effective transaction structure. Having ready an up-to-date RICS valuation of assets, debtors' books and realistic future forecasts in place will speed up the buy side process and help you sell your business.

Current management and staff are likely to remain significantly involved in the day-to-day management and operation of the business. They may also offer the owner a part-time consulting role or the opportunity to earn additional returns based on future performance. This often causes less business disruption and negative impact on customer loyalty and staff morale.

Although financial buyers may not actually have extensive knowledge of your sector, they can be very well connected and even have industry-specific advisors. This can lead to growth in the business and help you maximise the sale price if you are willing to stay on as a consultant and benefit from earnouts and deferred consideration.

Strategic Buyers

Strategic buyers differ from financial buyers in that they are interested in how a company fits into and drives their own long-term business plans. They are usually in a similar industry to you and do not want to acquire a business just for the cash flow. They seek to acquire businesses that complement the capabilities of their own business – or other businesses they already own. The reasons for acquiring your business may be the following:

- Entering new geographic markets
- Gaining new product lines
- Winning new customers or contracts
- Elimination of a competitor

- Acquiring new skills or abilities such as:
    - Sales,
    - R&D capabilities or
    - intellectual property.

Consequently, a strategic buyer is often willing – and able – to pay a higher price than a financial buyer.

The strategic buyer sees the target – your company – as an opportunity to acquire the elements that fit with or enhance their existing business. The reason for this decision is often that it is cheaper and faster to acquire an existing business than to build or develop your own business from scratch. This growth by acquisition is a common cornerstone of many growth strategies.

One of the best examples of this strategy happened in 1985 with the acquisition of a UK Manufacturer of wire shopping baskets and teapots called Wire and Plastic Products. This company has become one of the best-known names in Marketing Communications. If you have not figured out who this is yet, if I call it WPP, and say it was purchased by Sir Martin Sorrell as the foundation on which he built the empire in international advertising and marketing services, ring any bells? Today WPP is a world leader and home to some of the most admired and successful agency networks. Ever since WPP began its strategy of growth via acquisition in the 1980's it has gone on to buy dozens of companies every year. The acquisitions continued in the 1990's when WPP bought firms in the healthcare advertising, digital-marketing, online shopping, digital media, data management, retail and corporate consultancy, and sports-marketing industries. In the 00's the acquisitions jumped in value when WPP purchased Young & Rubicam Group for $5.7 billion, the largest takeover in the advertising sector and making WPP the largest advertising company in the world. In 2018 Sir

Martin Sorrell retired and was eventually replaced by Mark Reid who, amongst many other transactions, sold the original Wire and Plastic Products company which was the start of the empire.

…and not a lot of people know that!

These strategic buyers have specific goals in mind and reasons to buy. Be warned, the strategic sale is a long-winded affair involving lawyers, due diligence teams, and the sale can be expensive because of this. These deals can quite often collapse. Strategic buyers often want exclusivity periods of six months plus.

Telcos and Recruitment companies will want to buy revenue streams and save on the operating cost base, both have a positive effect on the value of a business.

In 1993 Chess ICT was founded, originally selling a water-management device. The business moved on to reselling gas and electric in 1995, followed by Telecoms in 1996. It was the Telecoms with a focus on business-to-business that then saw them make over 100 acquisitions for capability and customers. In 2010 they purchased Shaftesbury Systems, a telecom billing platform, expanding the service offering for their wholesale channel. To strengthen their mobile telephony offering, in 2014 they purchased Avenir Telecom, an O2 and EE distributer. One of the hardest things to get right with so many acquisitions is the culture and employee retention. Chess have been working on making sure they are a great company to work for and were awarded the 1st place in The Sunday Times best companies to work for.

Manufacturing companies will want to look at acquiring companies above or below them in the supply chain. This allows them to de-risk the supply chain by owning it all and also by bringing in-house the cash and profits generated by the company being acquired.

The retailer American Eagle acquired their fulfilment operator Quiet Logistics, a company that runs eight fulfilment centres across the USA for $350 million USD. Quiet Logistics also work with well-known companies such as Peloton, Away and Outdoor Voices. This became the second logistics acquisition for American Eagle who also acquired AirTerra, a shipping solution provider. This is quite a strategic shift amongst retailers as most retailers choose to outsource their logistics operations to third-party organisations. They are not the only retailer buying into their logistics supply chain. Right in the middle of the Covid Pandemic Costco bought the supply chain solution company Innovel Solutions for $1 billion. Meanwhile, Panasonic purchased the supply-chain software company Blue Yonder for $6.5 million.

Other companies, Investors and Private Equity companies will look to add value by building out a group. For example, WPP Group is a large holding company involved in communications, advertising and public relations. That reduces risk, helps grow a business horizontal across verticals or can be a way of buying in the resources or skillsets that are needed to grow.

Competitors may want to acquire your company to consolidate the industry sector and make them the biggest in the vertical space.

Maybe not the best example to write about as they were crippled by the covid pandemic. Pre-Covid, Cineworld Group PLC, the second largest cinema chain in the world, purchased Regal for $3.6 billion making it the top competitor to AMC. Cineworld's return on invested capital associated with the Acquisition expected to meet its cost of capital in the first full year after completion. The most intriguing element of the deal structure was the financing, and the acquisition costs were paid for via a rights issue. Also, due to the size of Regal, this deal was a reverse takeover under the listing rules of the UK Financial Conduct Authority. Basically, Cineworld added so much more value to the company it could just issue more shares to buy the

Regal cinema chain. Strategically the purchase of Regal allowed Cineworld to enter the largest box office market in the world. Being a public limited company, the shares are classed as liquidity, but private company shares are pretty much worthless and carry no value.

The strategic buyer will more often than not pay a higher price as they see the acquisition as a 2+2=6 scenario – with consolidation of business administration expense and improved buy price in the supply chain adding to the combined profitability.

Of course, there is no hard and fast rule, but there are two consistent reasons why strategists are generally willing to pay more. The main reason is synergy, which is the additional value created by the merger of two companies, creating opportunities that would not have been available to those companies independently. Synergy gains resulting from operational improvements are often used by acquirers to justify mergers – and the greater the value of perceived synergies, the greater the interest in your company and usually the higher the price. In short, the better the fit, the more they will desire the company and the higher the premium they may be willing to pay. On many occasions the price can be inflated due to the barriers to get to what you can deliver. For example, what price would you put on the amount of time it would take to develop your IP or get the volume of customers that you have?

Build your list of possible strategic buyers and highlight synergistic opportunities in your Information Memorandum. You may also want to produce more than one Information Memorandum; definitely do this if you are targeting both financial buyers and strategic buyers. The obvious points to consider are:

- Expansion of the customer base

- Access to new markets Geographic diversification

- Access to new brands
- Higher growth potential
- Squeezing a competitor out of the market
- Higher market share
- Experienced workforce
- Intellectual property
- Processes and Procedures
- Extended geographic reach
- Enhanced reputation
- Scale (greater influence with suppliers and customers)
- Lower operating costs
- Increased pricing power
- Access to distribution channels
- Increased turnover

One point of note, if you are going to target strategic buyers you will need to use a third party to keep yourself anonymous. You don't want your competitors, suppliers, or customers to know that you are wanting to exit as it could have a detrimental effect on your business. We offer a Strategic Buyer service that will not divulge who you are until after a Letter of Intent or Heads of Terms has been agreed.

https://www.GoSellMyBusiness.com/StrategicBuyers

The second reason why strategic buyers may pay more for your business is that they are usually larger companies with better access to cheap capital. And they often have another currency at their disposal: Shares. Strategic buyers often offer shares, cash or a combination of both as payment for the purchase price. They have more buying tools at their disposal than most financial buyers. It may be that they can just add you to their existing PLC with liquid shares by issuing more shares and reverse listing you on to the stock market.

You are more likely to fall foul of lengthy earnouts or golden handcuffs with strategic buyers offering some upfront payment and then a pot of gold at the end of the rainbow when targets are reached. However, future targets can be onerous and harder to achieve with new financial reporting meetings, reviews, audits, financial processes, corporate governance, and large company lethargy.

Entering the large corporate culture can have a detrimental effect on your business culture and morale with the bureaucratic paralysis. Although management may have improved promotion opportunities there will also be the risk of redundancies in duplicated roles. Your customers may be affected as their loyalty to you and your brand are diluted and the larger of your customers may now become a minnow. I know from more than one business that I have acquired that I have done a customer cull, removing low margin customers, small customers, and always removed the rude and disruptive customers.

We have recognised that finding your match is not that easy. Quite often when I speak to a business owner on who will buy their business, they come back with a list of three or four companies that may be interested. This is why we have put together a business buying and selling dating app service focussed on financial buyers and have put together a team of consultants who focus on the strategic buyers. The consultants will come from your industry and will already have connections, but more importantly they have been trained in the dark arts of building a buyers list and tailoring an Information Memorandum to titillate a buyer’s response. You can find more information on these services on our training course or by contacting us to discuss your requirements. Not all businesses fit in the strategic buyer's path, so call us to see if your business is suitable.

Part III: Exit Planning

Chapter Six: Intellectual Property

There are about 7 million SME businesses in the UK. Nearly 20% of new business fail in the first year and that rises to 60% by the end of the third year.

All business owners start out enthusiastic and positive that they will succeed and be able to retire or sell the business. They know it will take hard work and countless sacrifices to dream, plan and then struggle through the challenges in the hope it will all pay off.

I remember one company a lift/elevator design and installation business that was bought by two guys who were made redundant from one of the biggest companies in the UK. They raised finance to buy the company and for the operations. They also raised money for a swanky new office, brand new top of the range Audi's and gave themselves large salaries way in excess of what the business could afford. They were so enthusiastic that they would quadruple sales that they didn't care. No amount of hard work would have made that happen – they just didn't have the same levels of IP that the company they came from had nor the reputation. IP and reputation are very important and if you can quantify that in your Information Memorandum and your balance sheet, the value of your business will go up for a buyer.

The fact is that there are some companies that seem to effortlessly grow, attract loyal customers build brand loyalty, create amazing products and generate a ton of cash, whilst some will get by and the rest fall by the wayside.

There are a number of reasons business fail, but that is not the focus of this book.

Businesses need to provide real value and sadly most entrepreneurs are failing to build anything of value.

A company's set of accounts has a section specifically for Fixed Assets. Those Assets are then used by the business to generate the sales.

What do you think of when you read Fixed Assets? If you are only thinking of the following examples: a property, a machine, photocopier and a car then you really need to read this section.

Is your business the first business you have built? Is it complete, or have you cut a few corners or just been too busy to do so?

I have been working with an internet marketer recently and he has, surprise, surprise, a marketing background and had grown his business to the point where he was earning £27k per month. It was taking a toll on him because he was doing everything. His goal was to grow his business and scale first to £100,000k per month and then £1,000,000 per month, by coaching and helping others and paying for a business mentor, who had already reached the income goal. Similar to taking on a non-executive director or consultant for guidance. It was time to build the other 'Assets' needed.

Why are Assets Valuable?

As far as an accountant is concerned, an asset is any resource that a business owns or controls. The asset can be either tangible or intangible. Fixed Assets are physical assets a business owns that are used to deliver value to customers, whether that be a set of products or services. Fixed Assets include Buildings, Plant, Equipment, Computers and cars etc. Current Assets represent the stock held, Debtor book and Cash. Adding together the Fixed and Current Assets less current liabilities gives you the

Net Assets of a business. This represents the business owners / shareholders value, i.e. the Balancing part on the balance sheet.

Assets represent the value of the business, and they can be converted into cash if necessary. The balance sheet of a business represents the original value of the assets less a depreciation charge. This represents the business apportioning the benefit of the asset over its useful life. Or another way of looking at it is if you transfer to a bank account the amount you put through the books as depreciation for the asset, then in theory at the end of the life of the asset you will have enough cash to go and buy another one. The point here is asset values are based on the monetary value of the assets and are reduced over time. However, in reality that may not reflect the real value of the assets.

Take for example the business premises. If owned, the building would be typically written off over 40 years. You do not live in your house for 40 years and say it is worthless. It would, in reality, be worth a hell of a lot more. A financial buyer will be on the lookout for this scenario as the books might show a Premises worth £150,000 but with a RICS valuation could be worth £300,000. The buyer might then look to leverage the value and use a potential mortgage on the premises to release the funds to buy the business.

Whilst the premises is the obvious target, the same could apply to other assets. Any plant and equipment will be of various ages and states of repair. I am reminded of Only Fools and horses when Trigger says he has had the same brush the whole time he has had his job. Everyone laughed and said no way! Trigger's answer was the head had been replaced four times and the shaft twice... The point being that the asset, a brush, is still a fully functioning and delivering as required.

Therefore, when it comes to selling your business, you want to reflect the true value of the physical assets you own.

Up until now we have skipped over intangible assets. By definition, you cannot see or touch them. But they still exist, and a business is able to leverage them to generate value and additional revenue. The intangible assets could give your business the competitive advantage needed to win business over your competition. Intangible assets include things like computer programs, copyrights, goodwill, patents and trademarks. They also include financial assets; these will be financial investments, e.g. bonds and shares, in either subsidiaries or other companies.

Now, you may or may not have chosen to put all of the above on your balance sheet. But, if you want to realise the best value for your business, then you need to at least identify every possible asset and ensure they are documented as part of the Information Memorandum. Let's go and take a look at other types of assets you might want to identify and include.

Brand Assets

As an internet marketer the product is less important and can be your own or someone else's. What is key is your branding, marketing and follow up activities.

Jeans are Jeans are they not? Pop to Asda and pay less than 10% of the cost for a pair than you would have if you bought Armani Jeans. You are paying £10 for the actual Jeans and £100 for the name.

Brands can take on an identity all of their own. Choosing the correct name and any associated connotations will influence the acceptance and understanding. Richard Branson's Virgin Atlantic played on this in a campaign. Concerned that people would not accept an airline with the name Virgin, implying young and inexperienced the advert said: **"Virgin Atlantic, more experience than our name suggests".**

Brands define themselves with a philosophy and vision that sets them apart from the competition. If set up correctly, just describing what the company stands for should be enough to identify the brand.

Make sure this vision and philosophy is shared across all the company assets – the office wall, the employee handbooks, the company websites, marketing materials and any social media platforms you use.

It would be unrealistic to assume that every business can create a global brand. Just being able to stand out locally might be your goal. You can look to use Ambassadors or build brand value by association. Take the world of coffee. Supermarket shelves are no longer just filled with coffee jars but pods, ground coffee and beans. Without the advertising with George Clooney would Nespresso be the brand it is today? Probably not.

Take the local rugby club, the club sponsor is a successful property development company that now turns over £32m and their name is all over the billboards. By positioning yourself next to their name you can leap your brand awareness.

Market Assets

This is all about finding and targeting your customers. Your market assets should be geared to allow you to communicate clearly and quickly to your prospects and sell them the solution to their problems. You need to track the investment and return on these assets to make sure you are doing it better and at a lower cost than your competitors.

Which Market(s) are you targeting – Local, National or Global? Now position yourself and your solution as pivotal compared to your competitors in that market. Be clear about what you offer and why customers chose you. Remember people buy from people they Know, Like and Trust. Make sure the words you use to describe your solution are complimentary and are positive.

Breitling markets themselves based on Precision and Reliability. Some of my friends have a Rolex but always comment on the lack of accuracy. The clocks in a Bentley Continental are Breitling, reinforcing for me that was the way I should go (also my friends have Rolexes and I am an individual and not a sheep, so I did not want to follow in their footsteps).

How are you finding and selling to them – direct or via a partner channel model? Building your own direct sales model means you can control and influence the messaging as you wish, i.e. your own Instagram, YouTube Channel, Premises etc. You can also take on and get paid a commission or fee to promote complimentary products via your market channels.

By 'outsourcing' your route to market you are relying on the influencers or channel partners. They could disown you or change their loyalty, thus putting a chunk of your revenue stream at risk. But, if done correctly, it is a great way to accelerate brand awareness and to be successful via association with others.

KYC – Know your customer. The more you know about your customers, the more chance you have of securing loyalty and increasing sales. The best way to do this is to use a CRM system to build a comprehensive profile of your customers – what they like, what they buy and challenges faced. There are free options and expensive options for benefit you might derive. What I learned when starting out in business turnaround is you have multiple products and multiple customers. Time to put them all in a matrix and a tick in the box for what each customer currently buys. Now target every customer and cross sell the other products and services you have. Having lots of customers is also not necessarily a good thing. You want easy to deal with customers who come back for more and you make a profit from. If a customer starts to cost you money jettison them (nicely).

This is the key point here. Knowing your customer means understanding them, knowing what they want, how they like to be engaged. And then over deliver.

Product Assets

A business needs to identify a problem or want (buying is an emotional decision so a need is not enough. We all need to eat more vegetables. Broccoli is not everyone's choice so how about chocolate covered broccoli? Perfect, everyone loves and wants chocolate and it satisfies the need for a healthy centre...)

Companies that have a single product do not tend to last long. A customer will have started out as a prospect. You set the path and funnel for them to follow, enticing them every step of the way.

Starting as a prospect they will be researching a solution to the problem or want they have, so give them something for free as a sweetener. The next step is to offer them a low-cost proof point or introduction into the solution, then you position your core product or solution and finally a follow up offering for them as a key customer.

Taking our business as an example our mission and funnel process is as follows:

As a business owner you are interested in Selling your business but don't know how and we are here to help.

For prospects we have a website and access to the first chapter in our book – Go Sell My Business.

The low-cost entry is a chance to buy the book either on Kindle or Paperback, which introduces the process and provides some valuable insight in what to do and what not to do. (Keep reading).

The call-to-action points customers to our core solution. We offer a residential course on how to sell your business. Sit with like-minded individuals and learn the ins and outs of selling your business.

As a customer we can also offer to list your business for sale and connect with our network of investors looking to buy businesses such as yours. We have 2 options here – a preliminary basic listing and a full listing service where we would also set up matchmaking sessions with investors who are interested in your type of business.

Having the funnel process means you can measure the activities at each step of the way, and as with most things if you want to improve something measure it.

System Assets

Anyone interested in buying your business is going to want to walk in and have a look around at everything. They will also be looking at how reliant the business is on you as the owner. If you walk out the door will it be like a house of cards and all come crashing down?

They are also going to want to know what systems are used and how integrated they are. They will be looking to assess the robustness of the process, what controls are likely to be in place and whether additional improvements might be needed in the short term.

Business Processes

We bought a 40% stake in a Print Business. The business owners had a totally manual process supporting the order to cash process. When we did a spot check on a dozen orders we found the final invoices had not been raised for some of them and hence the overall sales revenues were down. Profit margins in the print world are already tight without an easily avoidable faux pas.

Even where the business systems and assets are set up and streamlined there can always be additional value derived.

We acquired 100% of another Print Business that had invested in software and had a slick process for taking enquiries, managing proofs, converting to sales orders and even tracking the budgeted costs for a job – so as to be able to track any actual inefficiencies or rework needed. The system was also sophisticated enough to track if the ideal machine was used, or a more expensive machine had to be used because of temporary lack of capacity on the main machine.

They had done the hard work to think about all the scenarios and best way to progress orders. But we identified they failed to realise they could claim R&D Tax Credits for the development and installation of the processes, that was a nice easy win for the cash flow, thank you HMRC.

Culture Assets

We are not talking about taking the team out for a wine and cheese evening or a night at the opera. We are talking about how the Human Resources function has moved on and rebranded itself as Culture and Talent and promoting compensation and benefits to the team.

An SME business may not even have an inhouse resource favouring an external agency for tasks as required. This makes the pulling together of Culture assets all the more important. At the end of the day every employer is looking to recruit, develop and retain the best employees.

Going back to my internet marketer, he had a philosophy of never doing a job or task more than three times. The first time you are doing it you are learning what to do, the second time you can refine that and look for improvements or look out for weaknesses caused later and the third time is very much getting it documented and outsourced.

Then once you have created the above step by step procedure the tasks need to be assigned to an appropriate role.

So, for each position or role you need to have a documented job specification. What needs to be performed, where to find the job guide and how the role is measured and compensated. And taking that one step further, having a set of job bands and salary scales for each job band.

As you grow the workforce you need to think about on-boarding programs, contracts of employment with carefully worded non-compete clauses, performance reviews, grievance procedures and sickness policies etc.

Tip: Non-compete clauses are always complex to enforce and you will want to avoid legal action.

The best one we saw was if you (an employee) leave and take a customer there is a flat fee of £x,000 for each customer that is poached. Similarly, if a course attendee subsequently sets up a course in direct competition, then a flat fee of £x,000 is payable.

The aim is of this chapter is to get you to think about Assets. Assets ultimately drive the value of a business and are used by the business to bring in the customers and deliver the quality products and services expected by them.

Making sure you are building something of value is vital. Documenting it for potential buyers to see shows clearly what is on offer. As a business owner it shows where you still have work to do to maximise the value of the business. Ultimately, the assets you build will allow you as the business owner to automate, step back and reduce the reliance the business has on you. This might help you transition from working in the business to working on the business. And the best bit, by having built the assets, you are adding value and also everything you have done will feed into the Information Memorandum pack you need to produce as part of the sale documentation.

Chapter Seven: Hiring Experts

Broker, M&A Advisor or Investment Bankers? That is the question. Whether it is nobler to suffer the slings and arrows of outrageous fortunes or angst against a sea of troubles.

A little poetic licence adopted but quite a fitting analogy. You should already know you need some experience or knowledge in how you go and sell your business; you have never done it before and maximised your exit value. Our courses are designed to give you the knowledge that you need to help sell your business but even after you have built the different packages in the Information Memorandum for your target audiences, you may still need some assistance in finding a buyer.

As previously discussed, a broker will package your business based on their predefined criteria. They will charge you for gathering the information and creating the information memorandum and putting it on their website and possibly a broker's aggregated website. The best way to understand what they do is not too dissimilar to selling a house. They will come to your property and have you sign a sole trader agreement. Even if you find a buyer or a buyer finds you, you will still be liable to pay the broker for years to come. The broker will prepare their own sales literature, normally their own templated Information Memorandum that they use for everyone. The broker will then add the information on their web site or a site similar to "Right Move" as an aggregator and then sit back and wait for a bite. The difference between an Estate Agent and that of a business broker is the Broker will want paying upfront. Now there is nothing wrong with being paid upfront for a job well done and there is a marketplace for a broker. But the broker is best suited for the micro business with turnovers less than £1m and £100k in adjusted profits including the owner's income or incomes.

The way the Broker produces the financial reports is based on an income and a job for a buyer. As we know a strategic buyer is looking for an investment and not a job. The broker will fudge the figures to create more value by taking out any of the owner managers salary under the justification that the owner will not be there after the sale. So, what has already happened is the Broker has alienated a massive segment of potential purchasers of your business or destroyed the potential of a better quality deal. A buyer who has some money and looking for a job won't necessarily see the manipulation of the profits of the business, but as the potential buyer gets into the due diligence their financial advisors will and the deals fall apart. The Broker will blame everyone else, but in truth having been in these situations it is more to do with the approach as to why the Broker has Broken the deal.

The Mergers and Acquisitions advisor will be a lot more proactive and more consultative than a broker. The M&A consultant will be a lot more strategic in planning your exit. They may lean on other specialists, either in their own practice or within their network of experts in building the strategy which can lead to several different flavours of the information memorandum. The M&A advisors will build a database of possible strategic buyers or may already be working with a group of strategic buyers. Nevertheless, the M&A advisor will be much more proactive than a broker, adding a lot of value on the way. This will often lead to higher prices and competitive bidding situations which will pay for itself rather than be an overhead.

The M&A Consultants will greatly differ from the more passive business broker, with the M&A Consultant having years of experience and may well have even bought and sold or be actively buying and selling businesses for themselves. Although their commercial offerings may vary, the normal is for some reduced level of consulting income upfront followed by a percentage of the sale. Expect to have some costs during the strategic 'getting ready for sale' and through 'the sales process'.

Even during the sales process, you can expect the M&A advisor to have a lot more enthusiasm for your business, a better eye for how to proactively market your business and be very keen in leading the negotiations and closing the sale. In comparison most brokers will setup calls and sit there in silence. The M&A Advisor is more likely to play a key role, not only in managing your data room and making sure the information quality is exceptional but will also help in making sure the information is complete in protecting you from legal warranties.

The M&A Consultant may have a background in business or finance, but not necessarily in your specific sector. However, they tend to have a world of experience. This is ok as they will often have the expertise for your specific business in their rolodex to call upon. The M&A Advisor doesn't need to be an expert in every business sector but does need to know how to strategically sell your business at a higher value, to the best new owners for your business. It is important that your marketing list is of prime quality and your information is also of the best quality. The broker's pitch is, "we already know the best people for buying your business" or "our distribution list is very large". How on earth would they know that at this stage? They don't know what makes your business great and what will make a strategic buyer want to acquire your baby. Think of the term "crap-in, crap-out".

Once a consultant has identified the best targets or built the target buyers list, they must have the skills and experience to present and promote your business convincingly. The purpose of the Information Memorandum shouldn't be to sell your business but not every advisor realises that. It should be a teaser for a buyer to have enough of a high-level picture to want to have the first call or meeting. We've seen large ring binders of documents sent out as part of a cold call email, which no one has the time to read, that give away far too much information for your competitors to learn about your business.

Our own M&A advisory service is designed for companies of all sizes. We can deliver experts in different fields and a buyside rolodex similar to what you might expect in a larger investment bank. Our à la carte approach allows for you to pick and choose from training courses to templates, deal rooms, deal teams to industry experts or even our strategic matchmaking service.

Adrian's Story

Adrian passed his Chartered Institute of Management Accounting exams but knew there was more to life and business than closing the books once a month, reconciling reports and explaining to department managers where their revenue and costs came from and how they could influence them.

As a Business Finance Analyst, he thrived in the fast-changing world of a growing Computer company, growing from £200m to £500m and then to £1Billion before leaving the day they announced their IPO.

He jumped across to become a management consultant, determined to deliver business benefits. This included reengineering business processes to incorporate best practices to remove bottlenecks and weaknesses and install ease of use, speed and control into them.

As a finance manager with a team of 12 he looked bored one day and one of his team said so, and that he had bought a buy to let property. Adrian asked how to do it and was told to read a book by Robert Kiyosaki. A month later he came in and told Adrian he had bought two more, was renting them to the local council and handed in his notice and was going to return to South Africa.

Adrian did all his research and got his ducks in a row to buy his first BTL property. His hand was shaking as he was signing at the solicitors and he was told, “this is your last chance to pull out,” and his reply was, “I’ve done my homework and I am ready for this”. That afternoon he stood in the property and the reality of being responsible for paying 2 mortgages set in. He went out and bought 5 more in the next 5 months and slept a whole lot better. Over the last 18 years of building a property portfolio he has had the misfortune of realising estate agents are mostly awful. They overvalue your house to blow sunshine up your arse to get you exited and they all have an imaginary list of active buyers ready to go. The majority sit there aggressively waiting for the phone to ring and then they show people round... this is the lounge (no shit, it has a big TV and a Sofa), here is the kitchen (again the cooker and sink give it away). Getting a buyer is one thing, but then also part of their remit is to do the sales chasing, help get the chain through the hoops to exchange and complete. Needless to say, the last one he dealt with proved they had learnt nothing about that process in the 20 years she had been selling houses!

There is a distinct correlation between estate agents and business brokers. Either it is the same type of person that does those jobs or they go on a special training course.

So as not to tar them all with the same brush, there are a handful of exceptions he could count on one hand that are good at their job.

He built his portfolio as a side-line but applied the same thought, research and delivery as in his day-to-day adventures.

Like Mark he spent years doing presales. Presales is all about understanding what a prospect is trying to achieve and understanding their pain points and what it would mean to them if the issues went away. Then identifying the solution or a range of solutions that will deliver the value. That could be information, amending a process or changing an approach. This is all about finding that win-win solution, preparing a plan to deliver that and then selling the value to both sides.

He used this approach to buy 3 businesses and then sold one of them. Again, it is all about understanding the processes and then bringing value to both parties that will get everyone what they want. His attitude and passion to deliver tangible results typifies qualities of great M&A consultants.

The investment bankers will be dealing in larger businesses of over £200m in turnover or unicorn businesses. The deal structures will be very different and will come from Venture Capital, PLC's, Investment companies or mature private equity firms. It may well not be a straight 100% sale but deal with an investment that can lead to an IPO or sector consolidation plays.

The investment banks, think of them more as a strategic transaction advisory service. They don't put their own money in to a business the same way that a retail bank would but rather seek institutional investors and investment houses.

On a traditional sale the Investment Banks will be very similar in the levels and quality of the work that you would get from M&A consultants, but you would expect to have a very large deal team of experts from the Investment bank. Many of the Investment Bankers in M&A that I know are all PhD level, specialist lawyers and financiers. You would also find some senior analysts on the team examining in finite details the strategic and financial fit for very large businesses that may be interested in buying your company.

Their access to facilitate an IPO to the markets is far greater than an M&A consultant and the Investment Bank will likely have offices all over the world. The level of the buyside they bring to the table can be on a global scale after presenting in global roadshows to large enterprise and institutions. But remember, the universe that the Investment Bank plays in is a lot smaller as they tend to be working on the larger publicly traded organisations.

The Investment Bank, as previously mentioned, can also initiate an IPO. An IPO can cost several million, a couple of million for the IPO and then a few more million for the Investment Bank to undertake a roadshow for potential investors. The cost of having a successful IPO can be too much for the normal business. However, an IPO can be a game changer for the shareholders in a business. It can deliver a massive capital event and allow them to continue growing their business by enabling them to go on their own acquisition journey with a new currency, liquid stocks on a main market.

Within our service offerings we can actually deliver a reverse IPO for smaller businesses allowing for a financial exit without you having to give up your baby.

Chapter Eight: The Deal Team

A team of one is not enough. For a successful deal to happen there are several job functions required with specific knowledge of M&A. You are already going to need to have a lot of time, energy, dedication, deal making process as well as learning the knowledge of how to do a deal.

You might have one or two people in your organisation that can help deliver everything you need to be able to get your deal across the line, but having a professional can make the difference. Consider all the functions required to successfully getting your deal across the line with maximum value creation. Do a SWAT analysis on yourself and what skills you have in your business. It is important that you are in the deal team even if you don't fulfil one of the roles.

The Deal Maker

Finding the right person for this key role is difficult. They must have experience, leadership skills, and negotiation skills. They must also be able to handle many tasks and deal with change. The role must also have sufficient knowledge on all aspects of deal-making and deal structure and most importantly know a lot about your business.

The person who fills this role will have a huge impact on the successful completion of the deal. If you aren't sure who this person is, you'll not be able to close deals for the maximum value.

If you want to be sure that your company has this critical role filled correctly, we can help! This person must have specific deal-making and investment negotiation experience and skills, as well as strong leadership.

Business Analyst

Companies need help in valuing their business to identify potential strategic and financial buyers. Identifying suitable buyers can be a difficult and time-consuming process. Potential buyers often have numerous considerations and interests that they must weigh against each other to determine whether or not they are a good fit.

Different people invest for different reasons, and you need to find a way to reach each one. Use a buyer persona strategy and create an investment thesis for each potential customer. Research the right messages to evoke an emotional response and convince them to take action based on your company and its offerings. Investment Thesis is a new way of creating marketing messages by using user personas, so you can communicate with financial or strategic investment audiences. It makes it easy to understand why they will buy from you and gives you a more effective way to reach them with the right offer.

Financial Analyst

Don't let potential opportunities slip through your fingers just because you lack financial understanding and the ability to present the financial information. The product or service you offer may be perfect, but if the buyer doesn't understand how to benefit from it, he'll not buy your business.

Every potential buyer wants to know how your business is different from others, how it stands out from competitors in the market, and why they should buy from you. Investors, both financial and strategic, are inundated with opportunities and spend a lot of time researching and analysing companies so they can make the most informed decision possible.

A good financial investment thesis is a must for any growing business. This important content should be one thing above all— convincing. It's not enough to just present an idea or a product if you're serious about making sales. With this powerful tool, you attract potential customers and build trust by meeting their needs with clarity and enthusiasm.

Communications

In the selling of the business the person in charge of the communications is like the Sales Rep, constantly titillating the deal. Keeping the communications going is tough but critical. Keeping your potential buyers engaged in conversation and avoiding the deal blowing cold during the months of the buying process can make or break a deal.

Contacting buyers, determining initial interest, negotiating and concluding an NDA, sending an Information Memorandum, following up to determine interest/progress.

Initiate in-depth discussions about the seller's business, assess mutual suitability, establish qualifications of potential buyers, build relationships, advance discussions, initiate discussions about valuation, establish parameters for client's business valuation (speak from position of factual evidence to support valuation parameters), establish synergies between client's business and investor's business, obtain written expressions of interest from potential buyers.

Negotiation of formal contractual terms (Heads of Terms) and initial deal structures. Managing exclusivity. Building out the data room and data requests/questions from the buyer. Ensure continued progress in drafting agreements and continued progress

Marketing & Information Memorandum

Creating a confidential Information Memorandum, teaser and all supplementary presentation materials takes time, effort and knowledge of research. You need specialists to edit with sales-promoting words and a touch of graphic design that appeals to the eye.

Lawyer or Legal Team

You are choosing a specialist lawyer rather than your ordinary contract or corporate lawyer. M&A lawyers assist their clients in the appropriate financing of mergers and acquisitions and advise them on the drafting, negotiation and execution of agreements for the sale of or parts of their business.

You will also need a CRM System

Managing buyer contacts and relationships can be a difficult and tedious task for someone with a busy schedule. There are so many time-consuming tasks that need to be completed at the same time, often resulting in forgotten emails, unanswered calls and missed appointments. To effectively generate new leads and manage relationships with existing leads, you need a CRM system that manages all your tasks automatically - from following up on meetings to setting alarms.

Above all, your deal team need to have strong negotiating skills. Every professional knows how important negotiations are. Whether you're a job applicant negotiating your potential salary or a top boss trying to close the next deal for your company, you'll have far more luck in your efforts if you master the art of negotiation.

If you want to negotiate a mutually beneficial agreement, it's important that you understand and appreciate what the other party wants to achieve with the deal. Wearing multiple hats, you can find out what's important to your buyer and offer a solution that's attractive and beneficial to both buyer and seller.

By asking: "What can I do to add value for the seller?", you shift the conversation from two-sided, where both sides lose, to cooperation, where both sides win. Together, parties can achieve more by openly sharing goals and defining what they consider a win. Negotiation is the art of hearing what's not being said and delivering that value in the deal.

Listening is the be-all and end-all. By actively listening and asking questions, you can find out what each party expects, needs and wants from the negotiation. In this way, a good connection with the other person is established and they feel heard and seen.

To be successful in your negotiations, it is very important that you streamline your communication. You can do this by using fewer words, knowing when to stop, and using the silent pauses. In fact, you need to get used to the pause so that your counterpart can digest the information and you can eventually come to a mutually beneficial deal.

Negotiation is a skill we use throughout our lives, including in many professional roles. If you find yourself in a situation where negotiation is required, follow the tips above related to communicating your intentions clearly, being curious, being prepared, listening, and reading cues while persevering through the potentially lengthy negotiation process. If you sharpen and follow these skills, you will have a great advantage in reaching a mutual agreement.

Chapter Nine: Premarketing

Marketing the business starts with an Information Memorandum. This is basically a sales brochure with the highlights of your business. Depending on who you are targeting to buy your business your Information Memorandum will have a specific focus on information that will attract that type of buyer. For example, your IM, if you are focusing on a US company to buy your UK business, will have statistics facts and information on the geography. Now, the same IM will not have the same appeal to a financial buyer who will be more interested in your financials, P&L, balance sheet, assets and anything else that they can leverage to raise finance against with which they can buy your business. Your goal is to also provide a potential buyer with the key facts that show the investment opportunity in the most favourable light. You do need to be careful to not overshare. Don't go putting down a list of customers – you don't know who is going to get this information from the Information Memorandum.

When I used to work for EDS, I remember once sitting in the British Midlands lounge at Heathrow waiting for my flight when three suits walked over to the nest of sofa's that I was sat at and asked to sit down. As they sat down I continued to read my newspaper but listened intently to their conversation. You see, it turned out that they all worked for Cap Gemini and were discussing how they were going to be pitching an outsourcing deal for a prominent Telecoms Company. Basically, whilst sat there, I learnt their whole pitch costings and profits. After they got up and left for their flight, I got on the phone and called up our top sales rep at EDS and relayed everything. EDS went on to win the business, we might have won it anyway but the insight really helped.

Just like the oversharing of information at the airport, we need to be careful about what information goes into an Information Memorandum. When we consult on a selling business, we always give the Information Memorandum a project name or code name. This way the exact business at this stage is unknown. Everyone should sign a Non-Disclosure Agreement, but that doesn't stop your competitors getting their hands on the information.

A good M&A Consultant will put together several different Information Memorandums with a different focus based on the type of buyer the information is going to be delivered to. The consultant will manage this initial stage for you and weed out the potential buyers that are not going to go the distance. You can find that you will get a lot of 'tyre kickers' who will think that they may be interested but they can waste time and fall away.

The preparation of the information memorandum is going to be the key to your success. Don't cut corners and don't think it's easy to put a presentation together, as there are many pitfalls and mistakes made. We cover a lot of what goes into an Information Memorandum in our courses and provide templates and examples, but when you take our Information Memorandum service, we always customise every single one. Just like your business is unique, they are never the same.

The Marketing Plan is quite simple:

- We create the Information Memorandums
- We build a target list of companies
- We promote the business directly and through our dating agency
- NDA's are signed
- The IM is distributed
- We hold an initial call with some Q&A

- We setup a call with the Business

- If finance is required, we introduce the buyer to finance

Our initial outreach programs are a summary or cut down version of the Information Memorandum. We condense the IM into one or two pages of highlights. We disguise the business with ambiguity, so it is near impossible to tell which business the IM is from. If the business is in Islington, London we would just say London. If the business is in Coventry, we just say the Midlands.

Yet many teasers about a business fail at this basic task. Look at 100 random teasers from 100 different brokers and you will probably find that at least 90% of them are just repetitive templates that they always use. Teasers are not just text; they are artfully crafted, eye-catching documents and emails designed to generate interest and convey a quality business for sale.

Think of the information flow like an engagement funnel for the basic 10 step plan:

1. First contact

2. Teaser Document.

3. NDA

4. Information Memorandum

5. Initial Call with Consultant

6. Call with the Business

7. Further information

8. LOI or Heads of Terms

9. Due Diligence

10. Sale and Purchase agreement

You will probably have a lot more steps in reality, site visits, information reviews, coffee’s, golf and dinners. It is a fluid sales process to get the buyer to say yes and deliver an offer in a Heads of Terms or Letter of Intent.

The IM is likely to be distributed internally by the investor to their team, and depending on the size of the buyer's company, is likely to end up on the desks of the Managing Director or the board members. This is an opportunity to put your best foot forward and ensure that the document contains a clearly defined opportunity, presented in a logical and compelling manner, highlighting areas of strategic synergies, unrealised potential and other investment priorities. Your document will be different for an investor than it would be for a corporate buying entity.

At every stage, you should leave the door open for more information, more questions. Just like in any sales process you are walking the buyer down a path, a question is a buying signal. Your meetings and conversations are about building rapport and trust in you. The buyer is going to need to work with you in the future, whether that be just in a hand over for a few months or in an earnout or reverse IPO. They are going to need to like you.

Never underestimate the importance of rapport building before you do anything else in the selling process. Here’s a little trick I used during lockdown, when all the meetings became webcam Microsoft Teams-based. I researched the investor/buyer, found out what they liked and changed my background image to match a hobby that we had in common. That could be a scuba diving image, skiing, the beach on somewhere they have visited. Facebook, LinkedIn, Instagram become the best rapport building tools around. Also, try and find out about their business and how they are run. You want to mirror as much as possible to create synergy. Remember to write all of this down in your CRM database.

What documents should you expect to deliver after the IM and initial consultation? A strategic buyer will want the last couple of years of Annual accounts. With covid in between, two years before and current. Don't be afraid of your covid accounts – everyone was in the same boat. A financial buyer will also want a complete asset register including when the asset was bought, original buy price and the value on the balance sheet. They will also need the current aged debtors and creditors. The financial buyer will want these as they will use this information to help raise finance. At this stage you should make the aged debtors and creditors anonymous; debtor 1, debtor 2, etc.

Get them ready before you start your sales process and keep them up to date. There's nothing worse than having to wait weeks and months for information as an investor or buyer. They normally have a low attention span and will run cold.

Some investors will want to have a list of your competitors and a high-level swot analysis. They want this to see what other companies they could buy to compliment your business with another acquisition or merger.

Accountants or other financial advisors may also want to see the Corporate tax returns and VAT returns along with any Tax relief and or R&D Tax Credits.

Expect a site visit. This can be on evenings and weekends if you don't want the employees to get suspicious. Make sure your workshops, stores and offices have been decluttered and look like a smooth operating environment. Don't have dogs and cats in the offices. Although it can have a nice, homely feel to the business, most new owners will prefer a professional corporate environment.

Now for the golden rule. Do not fall into the broker's trap of exaggerating and fabricating information to make yourself look better. Stick to hard facts and avoid marketing spin.

Information Memorandum templates
https://www.gosellmybusiness.com/IM

Chapter Ten: Due Diligence

What is Due Diligence or you may just hear it called DD? Due diligence documents are the investigation and analysis of a company or organisation conducted in preparation for a business transaction. Due diligence documents typically include the following categories: Corporate, Legal, Government and Legislative, Finance, Property and Assets, Sales and Marketing, Customer and Supplier Contracts, and Human Resources. You may have other documents which are important to the buyers influence such as ISO standards and the relevant documentation

If you are selling your business, there are several advantages to having first-class due diligence documents prepared in advance. The very process of putting these documents together gives you a good overview of your own business and where some of its potential weaknesses lie. As long as the business has not yet been sold, or in negotiation you can work towards strengthening the areas that your due diligence documents indicate need strengthening.

On the buyer's side, receiving these documents in a timely and proper manner speeds up the M&A process and gives you confidence that what's under the bonnet matches what's in the company's Information Memorandum marketing materials. Most importantly, it is the best signalling mechanism a company has to show that it is worth acquiring.

Why is setting up a due diligence such a headache? It is a lot of work collating documents, contracts and agreements etc. The information requests can start quite early on in the process when someone starts to ask questions and requests clarification on items in the Information Memorandum. Some of the most common questions requested are the Asset Register, Debtors Book and Creditors book – two of which are fluid and change daily. It is easier to collect and keep track of all the documents and files needed in one place rather than emailing in dribs and drabs. This location in the Mergers and Acquisitions world is called the Data Room.

We have a data room offering to make your life easier which can be integrated into Windows Explorer or used on the web. It is simple enough to use and share, but we also have training materials for you to use and templates in word and excel to make your life easier. We also have a simple process for buyers to register for access along with a 'non-disclosure agreement' to sign before they are granted access.

1 Due Diligence Corporate Documents

The corporate documents are all the legal information relating to the formation of the company. It is a very high percentage of companies that I have looked at that I have found have errors in the legal documentation. Putting the corporate documents together early can help identify mistakes that have been made in the past before the sale. Mistakes in good faith that I have seen that could cost you dearly are simple things like not removing or transferring shares from previous employees, directors and shareholders. If you have made mistakes or another professional has made mistakes, believe me when I say, I have seen accountants make some mistakes in the basics of share capital allocations.

Remember in chapter one when we discussed having someone who knows what they are doing, performing that role? In one company that I was looking at they had share listing as Ordinary Shares from A through to E. One of the original shareholders was wanting to sell his shares to his son and retire. It is a bit of a habit that I have to look straight away at the shareholding to see who has what as far as voting rights and check the Memorandum and Articles of Association. It was then that I noticed the company had originally started with just 1000 Ordinary shares and at some point suddenly started with the

Ordinary Shares from A through to E. When you create shares in the UK you do that through a special resolution and a Companies House SH01 for a return of allotment of shares along with the prescribed particulars. Also, when you remove shares, in this case the Ordinary Shares, you need to submit Companies House Form SH06 Notify a cancellation of shares. The shares also must have 'prescribed particulars'. This sets out what the shares have rights to do, for example voting rights, and most importantly for this company, rights to dividends. The trusted friend and their accountant had created all of the Ordinary Shares from A through to E and allocated himself Ordinary E without all the correct forms. He also, when creating all the share classes, only put on the prescribed particulars voting rights. This meant that over the years no one was intitled to dividends, including himself. In this situation it wasn't much of a problem and the error could be easily corrected. But, if the company had failed and gone into administration, the administrators would be entitled to ask for all the disbursements back from the shareholders who were not entitled to them.

With all that in mind, you will want to gather all the information and have a professional look over them before they are published. Most buyers are ok if mistakes have been made, as long as they have been fixed, legally, before completing.

2 Material Agreements

It will be important for the buyers to have a good understanding of the commitments of the business and the terms and conditions that the business is committed to. Whilst putting together the documents, you should highlight the specifics such as start and end date, and if it is a finance agreement, the interest rate. It might be that the buyer may want to look at the asset leases with a view to refinancing the business assets and the termination clauses will be important should they want to replace the agreement with an extension or a facility with better rates.

The lists and types of agreement that you will need to get together here are quite extensive. You will need to make sure you deliver everything as these agreements will form a large part of the buyer's legal due diligence and be evidenced in the warranties. Our due diligence pack, data room and training will cover everything that you will need to put together. It may be you don't have the original documents such as bank mandates for example, so you will need to ask for them yourself.

3 Legal and Litigation

Also within legal due diligence is a process used to assess the legal risks involved in a merger or acquisition. It requires lawyers to record, understand and assess the legal risks associated with a prospective acquisition. The lawyer will be looking at any past litigation or disputes, any possible current or future issues that may occur. Given that the representations and warranties made by a seller in relation to the purchase of your business in a sale and purchase agreement are limited to the extent of disclosure to the buyer prior to the sale, you have a material interest in ensuring that the documents provided to the buyer in the data room are as comprehensive as they are accurate and give a true picture of the legal position of the target.

You will need to list of all suits, actions, litigation, administrative proceedings and investigations or inquiries by or affecting the Company or any of its properties or assets, including, without limitation, any civil, criminal, administrative, arbitration or other similar proceeding or investigation, pending or threatened. In each case provide summaries, including parties, nature of proceedings, date of commencement, current status, relief sought and estimated actual cost, insurance coverage, if any, and any legal opinions rendered in connection therewith and an assessment of the merits thereof and copy of relevant documentation including emails.

All orders of courts, administrative agencies or other tribunals or of settlements imposing continuing obligations or restrictions on the Company or any director, officer or employee. All notices or demand letters received during the last five years relating to any claims against the Company in respect of services rendered, with respect to which no litigation has yet been filed. Sometimes these demands just go away but they can come back under new management or administration. It will be prudent to have a summary of disputes with suppliers, competitors or customers.

4 Employees and Contractors

In the first instance a buyer will want to see an org chart. You should also have any empty boxes on the org chart where you are looking to recruit into or where the team is currently light. You should also highlight anybody who is thinking of leaving or is likely to go on paternity or maternity leave.

Who are the most important employees and how do you think they would react to a sale?

How will you retain the employees after the sale?

What questions will your buyer ask about employee retention?

Look at it from their perspective.

Should you tell your employees that you are looking to sell? It doesn't really matter how close you are to your employees, you treat them like family, they are family, people don't like change. They can be fearful of the change and then whisper amongst themselves. If one person mentions that there is a risk of redundancies after the purchase, all of a sudden everyone is looking for a new job. In companies whose employees belong to a union, this can spark trouble and scupper a deal. You will need to inform the union when the deal is ready to sign, the union will want assurances for the employees in the agreements to mitigate the personal risk to the employees and you will need to include the buyer in the negotiations to mitigate any risks a buyer might face.

The buyer is going to want to see all of the employment related contracts, employee benefits, employee handbooks, policies, grievance procedures, insurance and job reviews. They will also want to see any employment related litigation and tribunals from the past and if there are likely to be any in the future.

5 Financial Information

Quite obviously the buyer will want to see detailed financial statements. Normally they will want three years previous financial information and current management information. They may want a business plan.

There's a story that I heard about a company that wanted to sell. They put together, as part of their business plan, a 30+ action plan that could improve the business. They thought that if they implemented the plan the business would have more value. In reality, to execute 30+ changes in a business would probably destroy the business, cost a massive amount of resources and funds and with most plans having a long range breakeven, take a long time to get back to the forecasted profits. The most valuable part of the 30+ action plan would be to include it in the Memorandum and business plan and leave it for the new owner. If you want to stay on, you could offer to implement a couple of them that the buyer wants to do. It will be the buyers' choice, not yours, which they want to do.

The buyer may request that the company financials are audited if the size of your company warrants financial audits or a smaller audit if your turnover is smaller. Or they may want to see historic bank statements to make sure the financial reports match what was posted as official accounts. Buyers know that the accountant will adjust so you pay less tax. So, it is advisable to know what they are so you can pre-empt any questions. Likewise, if the Information Memorandum doesn't match the figures produced to end of year accounts the buyer will ask questions, so get them ready.

There are a lot of areas in financial due diligence that we have not touched in this book which are available in the various training courses that we provide. Or if you need assistance with due diligence, we can recommend specialist consultants that will assist in building your due diligence data room.

6 Real Estate Property

This is straight forward to produce. It is simply a list of properties owned, leased or rented by the company. Now you need the next level of detail – Title deeds, mortgages, leasehold mortgages, deeds of trust and security agreements relating to the properties listed in the preceding paragraph. All outstanding leases and tenancies with an original term of more than one year for real and personal property where the Company is either lessor or lessee. You should also detail any improvements to the property since originally purchased or leased and if the accountant has included this in the management accounts.

If the property was purchased by the business, then it is owned by the business. If the property is owned in your pension or SIPP, then you will need to get a professional valuation undertaken if you want to sell it or get three local commercial agents to give an appraisal for the market value in creating a lease agreement. Plucking a figure from the sky or insisting that the new buyer pays a rent that is over-valued because the business has paid it before is not realistic. This will turn a buyer away, so be prepared, you may actually be under valuing the property.

7 Plant and Machinery

You will also need a robust asset register with the backing of a professional valuation. In the UK the valuer should be a RICS valuer. Your accountant should know of a professional valuer, if not reach out to us and we can put you in touch with a valuation expert for your sector. The asset register will be of significant importance to a buyer as they may look at utilising the assets in some form of lending to purchase the business. When we owned a print business we looked for another one to bolt on and we were keen to assess the age, scale and capacity of the machines to see whether we could offload or replace some of the old machines or end the leases early. Your annual accounts should already display the depreciation or amortisation methods used, but if they don't, check with the accountant and get a letter in writing from them for the due diligence reports.

You will also need any maintenance and warranty agreements for the hardware and licence agreements for software. Include all the equipment and highlight any equipment that is leased and end of life that needs replacing. If it does need replacing it would be a good idea to get some quotes ready and lease agreements – should the new owner want to go ahead with replacing the items prior to purchase.

8 Intellectual Property

IP in a business could have some significant additional value. If you have the IP in a separate company and licence it back to the company, you should get a professional IP lawyer to look at the licence and the ownership rights. List all trademarks, service marks, slogans, trade names, trade dress or logos ("**Marks**") in use by the Company and any registrations of such Marks. If the Marks are used only in common law, identify the first date of use and the provinces, states and/or countries in which they were used. Copies of all licenses or other agreements establishing such interests or rights. You may have documents processes and procedures which should be copyrighted. Now is a good time to get that done.

There may be other IP which you licence to use in the business, certainly most software is a licence to use the IP. So, any software you have in the business make sure you have the agreements in place.

9 Taxation

Compile a list of your corporate tax returns for the last 5 years. Your VAT or local sales tax returns. Employment tax returns. You will need to evidence that your Company is current on sales tax, unemployment, social security, and other tax payments.

If you have filed any R&D tax returns you will need to provide the R&D reports and backup evidence. If you have used a third party to create and submit your R&D returns you will need to provide all copies of files and communications to support all the claims.

10 Insurance

Provide copies of all insurance documentation. Summary of insurance policies relating to the company, its assets and its business. All material insurance policies of the company covering its assets, liabilities and operations.

Existing insurance policies, such as "key person" policies and the calculation of the cash value of those policies. A list of pending claims and disputes with insurance companies and details of denials of cover. Any other relevant documents relating to the company's insurance and liability risks, including special reserve funds and accounts.

11 Acquisitions, Partnerships or Joint Ventures

List any current, past or potential acquisition, partnership or joint ventures. These can be valuable to the person who is buying your business as they may already be thinking about some sector consolidation and acquiring similar businesses that look like yours.

If you have never thought about or tried to engage in an acquisition strategy, partnership or joint venture arrangement, start by creating a list of your local and regional competitors.

12 Environmental

Depending on the sector of business you are in, an environmental report may be needed by a qualified person. If you are in the motor trade then you should be including policies for disposal of spent oil, old tyres and what to do if you have a spillage. If your business does have any form of environmental governance, then include:

Communications to and from environmental regulators, including notices of violation.

Correspondence with environmental authorities in the last three years.

Environmental audit and inspection reports from the last two years.

Documents relating to environmental liabilities arising from an activity in the last five years. Any knowledge of previous uses that could lead to further investigation of negative environmental impacts.

13 Government regulations

Many businesses will not need to compile anything in this section, but if your business is under any form of regulations, licence or special permit, then list all permits and licences, along with expiry dates. If there are any licences under your name only to operate — as may be the case in the haulage industry — then these risks need to be highlighted. If there are any licences and permits that are under your name for the business, then you should come up with some risk mitigation plans.

14 Supplier and Customer Contracts

Here you list all the contracts and agreements along with start dates, end dates and values. You should also highlight your top 10 customers and suppliers with a percentage of turnover or spend. This will be useful in developing a risk mitigation plan in handing over the business and the relationships that need to be maintained. You might want to develop a communication plan with the potential purchaser on how best to approach your customers and suppliers when the time is right. Just like with employees, you don't want to spook your customers as they may look to move on under the risk of losing a supplier. It is very important to create a solid communication plan to implement during handover.

Due diligence is important, it may be labour-intensive and laborious, but it needs to be done. Our training course on due diligence, our templates and data room will help you take a giant leap.

https://www.GoSellMyBusiness.com/DueDiligence

Chapter Eleven: Deal Structures

What is a deal structure? Putting it simply, a deal structure is based on what is being sold and how it is being purchased. Purchasers very rarely turn up with a wheelbarrow full of money and make a payment with cash up front. Investors and Buyers are typically experienced and could be more creative. Having an idea of what might be presented and understanding the mechanics of each will help with understanding of the deal price and methods in negotiations. The purchasers deal structure will be based on breakeven and risk mitigation in the transaction.

Obviously, you want the most you can get. Buyers want to pay the least amount of cash out, but that does not necessarily mean the total value offer needs to be low. It could be made up of some cash, some shares, deferred payments or even an earnout based on future profits.

So let us look at some of the structures we have seen offered and have indeed used ourselves.

We are making an assumption here that the business is profitable and a going concern. For distressed businesses it is more a case of giving the business a hospital pass, a last chance at survival and helping the business owner get off the hook for any personal guarantees.

LBO – Leveraged Buy Out

A leveraged buyout is often part of an M&A (Merger and Acquisition) strategy and can be used to acquire competitors or enter new markets; enabling a company to diversify its portfolio. Buyers like leveraged buyouts because they do not need to put up a lot of their own money. The business being sold is usually well established and profitable and if it has debt that figure is low compared to the overall business assets.

Why would a target company want to sell via an LBO?

This is a common way to sell a business. The seller can get the price they want for the business and have a way to exit the business with a solid plan. A leveraged buyout is an ideal exit strategy for entrepreneurs who want to cash out at the end of their career, as much of the final offer could be an immediate cash payment.

The buying company will then use the cashflow from the day-to-day sales to fund and paydown the debt that was taken on to pay off the business owners. Therefore, the cashflows and gearing levels of the debt are all key to ensuring the business can survive and thrive over the coming years.

A famous LBO deal that you may well be familiar with is when and how the Glazers purchased Manchester United football club. The deal was based on an asset backed loan of about £600m secured against the club's assets (the stadium, land, etc). They also had another £200m loan; a PIK loan secured against the shares in the club. They later refinanced some of the loans by raising £500m in a bond issue. All the Glazers had to do to pay for all of this was to raise ticket prices by £15 to have no impact on the club. There has been a lot of restructuring and refinancing of the debt over the years, but this is the basics of how an LBO deal works.

On the course we go into the details of the types of assets that can be leveraged and by how much.

Vendor Finance

Vendor finance is a form of lending in which a company lends money that the borrower uses to buy the business. Vendor finance is usually taking the form of deferred loans from the seller or shares subscribed by the vendor. Often the seller takes shares in the borrowing company. This type of financing is usually used when the vendor's expectation of the value of the business to be higher than the buyers, and there is then room to negotiate the interest rate on the borrowing, based on the risk associated with transaction.

Vendor finance bridges the valuation gap created by the time value of money. If the buyer of a business does not have to repay the seller back for a few years, the value of that part of the purchase price is worthless. In some cases, the seller's loan accrues interest, in other cases it is simply a deferred payment. Vendor finance is different from an earnout because it is not contingent on any specific business performance metrics.

Vendor finance might be used when the buyer does not have all the funds to buy the entire business. In this case, the vendor provides an interest-bearing loan to help the buyer complete the purchase and help the seller complete the sale, usually on better terms for the seller.

On the course we go into arranging finance with an agreement that if the loan is not repaid, not only are there interest and recovery charges but there is a clawback of the shares to the business. The original owner might not want the business back but if it means he can get it back and have a chance to sell it again it provides a way of mitigating the risk of non-payment.

Deferred Consideration

In its simplest form, this is as it sounds. A buyer will want to pay some up front and want to pay the balance later.

Deferred consideration could be a one-off or might be structured as 6 monthly or annual payments over 2,3,4 or more years.

We have heard it many times – be happy with the initial payment as there is a risk that over time, for whatever reason, the deferred consideration may not be paid. Sometimes the deferred payment becomes a resented payment. The seller may not want to stay to get the payment and the buyer does not want to continue to pay the old owner for having sailed off into the sunset. Enforcement of the payments can become a challenge and could cost thousands to get to court in the hope of a clean settlement.

We will be explaining on the course how to mitigate that risk using debentures, bonds and preference shares.

Deferred Consideration can also take the form of Earnouts.

An earnout is a future payment that is based on a performance metric. Say for example based on revenue and profit. If the business hits a 5% growth year-on-year and maintains its profitability level, then there will be an additional payment made to the previous business owner.

When Matt sold his software company, he had two offers on the table. The first offer was significantly more but was structured heavily towards deferrals and earn outs, but he lacked the confidence in them to deliver so he took the other offer, which was $10m. The first $6m was payable up front on signature in the form of cash and shares in the acquiring company (listed on the stock market), a figure of $2.1m was deferred over 3 years and the balance based on sales targets achieved for his old company's software solution over the same 3-year period. Matt had chosen to stay with the business as well, thus the handover was easier and was able to continue to drive the solution forward globally and influence the growth to ensure the earnouts were achievable.

MBI/MBO - Management Buy In / Management Buy Out

A management buy-in (MBI) is used to describe the scenario where an investor, manager or an independent management team raises the necessary finance to buy a company and joins the board or becomes the new management team. The benefit to you as a seller is a management buy-in team is often not alone in looking for suitable targets to invest or buy into. This will help maintain the value of your business or maybe increase it.

From the softer side of your sale, you may want the comfort that the new management team is fully invested in your business and will not only say they are keen to pick up your business and move it along but they will usually have a significant amount of experience, meaning once you sell, your former baby will be in safe hands.

The difference between an MBI and a Management Buy-out (MBO) is in the position of the buyer. In an MBO there may be a director or management team that wants to pick up the reins when you are looking to exit. You already know them; they already know your plans and strategy of the business. That can be an advantage. You may already have a succession plan in mind or know there may be a willing successor. You are then in the perfect position to nurture that and help structure the deal in a mutually beneficial way for both parties.

There is a hybrid alternative to the above called a BIMBO. No, it's not what you are probably thinking. Buy-In Management Buy-Out. This is where the internal management team and an external investor / director join forces to buy out the existing business owner.

Main Market Shares

Selling your business may not be your dream. You want to take your company Public and get it listed on one of the leading stock markets. Dreaming of ringing the bell on the trading floor when the market opens on the day your IPO becomes a reality?

As a shareholder in a privately owned business the shares that you own in your business are illiquid. That means you will find it very difficult to sell some of your shares if you needed to raise some cash. Likewise, if someone were to buy some of your company shares as an investment, they too would find it difficult to sell them. There is no marketplace to buy and sell shares in SME businesses.

IPO - Initial Public offering

Let me set your expectations. Going down the IPO route will cost over £1million in fees. Read that again. Going down the IPO route will cost over £1million. Very few start-ups will get to the scale and profitability that will take them to that route.

In 1998, I resigned from working as a lowly finance business analyst for Computacenter, just as it announced its floatation on the London Stock Exchange. The floatation released a boat load of cash for the owners Philip Hulme and Peter Ogden. I had already been fortunate enough to spend a day on Peter's boats. The morning was spent on a Sunseeker, riding the waves, powering through the wakes of other boats. Then came the drenching for those unfortunate enough to be sat at the back of the boat when we dropped the speed allowing the stern wave to catch up and come over the back of the boat. The afternoon was more sedate, relaxing in the sun on the deck of the yacht watching the world drift buy, this time under sail and a chance for those a bit soggy to dry out.

IPO's do not need to be in the Billions as with Porsche's IPO €75.2billion (911 million shares). They have a ton of regulatory requirements that need to be met on a regular basis.

AIM Shares

AIM is the Alternative Investment Market and is a submarket of the London Stock Exchange. It is designed for smaller cap companies who want the ability to release funds and secure investment without the all the expense and tight regulation requirements of the main markets. The AIM market doesn't have the same levels of liquidity as main markets so transactions are a lot lower. The AIM market also does not have the same sort of attraction to the institutional investors so buying and selling shares can often be difficult.

Share Swap

Ok, so a floatation is not for everyone. I am wanting to sell my business so why would I want to do a share swap? There are two types of shares swap we will consider here. The first is a straightforward share swap where you sell your company and in return some or all of the consideration is shares from the buying company. The second is what is called an Agglomeration. Agglomeration is a trademarked term that we will elaborate on in a minute.

Straight Share Swap

You sell your company to another company. Part of the deal might be in shares. You are selling your limited company shares for those in another limited company. It is unlikely the whole deal will be in shares. But ask yourself why would you swap your shares and control in your business for shares in a business where you have little or no influence in?

Any buyer who has access to a shareholding in a company may consider using those shares as a way to finance the acquisition of a business. That means less cash outflow and also potentially might consider a slightly higher valuation as at the end of the day both the buyer and the seller need to assess what the value of the shares are and the valuation of the acquirer, based on what they expect to be the valuation of their company. Offering the outgoing owner / shareholder shares and possibly share options in the acquiring company looks to tie in the owner. They will benefit in the long term with dividends and an increase in share price.

Both could be seen as downsides by the seller. When we acquire a stake in a business, we want to see there is a clear dividend policy. For us, ideally the dividend policy says 80% of retained earnings each year are distributed via profits. That ensures all the shareholders know why they are investing and why they add value, and the remaining 20% ensures sufficient cash flow for the ongoing business. If additional funds are needed for investment purposes there is an open conversation to be had over the strategy, the cost and investment required. Just relying on the share value to increase as a way of getting a payback just adds risk. Will the share price increase? Some sellers will want the ability to sell some or all of their shares in the future for whatever reason. They therefore look for a buy-back option and whether there is a good level of liquidity in being able to trade the shares is key factor for sellers. For some sellers, being paid as a non-executive director or a chairman position in addition to a cash lump sum as part of the deal structure will be a deal maker. Others will want to ensure that any deal on the table offers any real value to any offer for sale. Personally, if I was looking for an exit then I would not be looking for a straight share swap. For me to consider that, it would have to be a small part of the deal pie. I would also want the share purchase agreement to contain drag and tag rights. That way, if I could find a buyer for the business as a whole, then I have my exit - either the existing business owner would buy me out or if the business owner thought it was a great deal, we would both be bought out by the new business buyer. Either way I get my exit.

Agglomeration.

Instead of swapping shares in your Limited Company for another Limited Company as in the above scenario, what would you think if you were able to swap your Limited Company shares for shares of a Publicly traded company listed on one of the major Markets?

We work with the board of a PLC listed company that look to acquire mature profitable businesses that would benefit from joining them as part of publicly traded company.

The agglomeration model was created to solve the problems entrepreneurs face in growing their businesses and creating value. Why should the rules for SME's be different from the big boys? An Agglomeration model combines the best elements of a traditional M&A roll-up with the benefits of an IPO and so is fundamentally a public listed company exclusively for the use of the SME.

When we reverse list the limited company into the agglomeration PLC the original business owner is offered a Board Position, assuming they want one. The value of their company is offered as shares in the publicly listed company. This gives them a liquid position so they can sell some or all of their shares if they want to release some cash. There is a tie-in for the first year. This ensures the business is genuine and will continue as the predictions expect, but also so a business owner does not just dump his shares and thus adversely affect the share price.

To be considered for the agglomeration model a company needs to be financially stable and profitable. Due diligence is performed, an Information Memorandum needs to be in place and succession planning needs to have been reviewed to ensure the long-term viability of the business joining the group.

You are probably now asking what else is in it for the business and ultimately the group?

The former limited company business will have access to the economies of scale based on the group, buying power and the ability to borrow for expansion at lower competitive rates or via bond listings. This is a real benefit to larger companies.

Closer to home the limited company owners now have access to a plc board that can help guide them in their business. "No man is an island" or "a problem aired is a problem shared". This means you no longer need to solve every problem; there is now an extended team, some of whom may already have come across and solved your problem or failing that have some input that might prove valuable. There will also be synergies in the group, so if it means the limited company can buy goods and services from within the group it means the profit on those trades remain within the group. This all adds to the overall profitability of the group and a subsequent increase in overall shareholder value.

In our opinion, why should an SME not benefit from the same level playing field the bigger cap companies get to enjoy?

At the end of the day, you as the business owner want to sell and have to accept that whilst you can negotiate some protection into the deal for the existing employees, it will be up to the new owners how they want to run the business. Your priority is to get the best possible deal you can.

Chapter Twelve: Closing

Lawyers and Legal Fees

It is not always necessary to involve a lawyer when drawing up the paperwork for the sale of a business. The foundation of any legal agreement is based on the following:

- Intent of both parties – The buyer wants to buy and the seller wants to sell;
- What is on offer;
- Acceptance of the offer and
- Consideration or what will the seller receive.

Lawyers will always tell you that they can or will only act for one side. There is nothing stopping the buyer and the seller agreeing what each party wants and agrees to and then both sitting down with a lawyer to draw up the document that incorporates all the terms.

Legal fees are always an interesting topic, as Lawyers only have one thing to sell, their time. Lawyers usually bill based on time, although on the odd occasion you can get a fixed cost fee arrangement. The Lawyers will track and charge for every call, email or even thinking time while acting for you. The longer that they can string out negotiating a deal and the more questions they can raise, the more money for them. But does that really add any value to tying up business sale?

An investor we helped bought a manufacturing business from the owner who had hit 70 and was looking to sell, as his wife wanted him around to enjoy their retirement together. He was advised to use a lawyer on a fixed fee basis, but instead opted for the time and material option. Needless to say, the sale took 3 months longer than normal to complete by the time that solicitor had finished asking countless questions. The Investor paid his lawyer a fixed fee of £8,844. The business owner had managed to rack up a whopping £39,860 in legal fees, a figure which shocked the seller. He even then had the nerve to ask the investor for a contribution towards the fees! I won't tell you how that conversation went, but the sale was completed.

Whether or not you choose to use lawyers or not and whether you opt to go down the fixed fee or Time & Material fee-based approach is down to you and your level of risk and comfort.

Either way, there will be a number of documents to be prepared, ready for the signature of both parties. There will be at least 2 key documents to sign. With the sale of the Chrome Plating business there was a complete trestle table full of documents printed in duplicate for each party to sign and countersign.

Heads of Terms

The Heads of Terms document is to assist in the identification of critical issues as early as possible during the negotiation of the sale. Setting out the basics and starting the open dialogue means a better chance of the sale going through.

The Heads of Terms is usually touted as being a non-binding document that outlines the main points relevant to the purchase and sale, but more often than not becomes binding as the contents become incorporated into the negotiations as both sides set out their stalls.

The template we use breaks down into the following sub-headings:

Parties to the agreement

Always useful to know who the contracting parties are; do they have the authority to enter into an agreement?

Statement of Intent

Intent is one of the four elements needed for a contract. That is exactly what you want. You want to sell your business and someone else wants to buy it.

Background

Over several meetings you will get to know the owners and the business. It is important to document and keep a record of what is shared. You need to understand what you are buying and your due diligence will seek to add assurance and comfort about the business and what you have been told. In here we like to document any values from the accounts and any adjustments that have been made to the figures shared, versus those filed in the public domain.

Proposal

SME company directors often take on personal guarantees as their business grows and they need to either lease equipment, extend finance or whatever it happens to be. The outgoing owner is going to want to see these removed or protected against, so they get a clean break. The proposal could cover this

Is the proposal to purchase some or all of the shares in the company? Under what conditions and terms does the selling party want to remain involved (or the extent to which a hand over period is negotiated)?

Obligations of the Seller

Oh Boy... I won't shame this individual, but he needed to sell his business. The business had been struggling and was in need of some assistance to turn it round. The negotiations had gone well, and everything was being written up to close the deal and then...nothing. He had gone on holiday at the drop of a hat thinking "job done" and everything was going to be fine. Well, it would have been if he had done what he needed to, but the paperwork was never signed, and the turnaround could not start. Mentally he had resigned as director but not actually signed the paperwork and when he did return, it was too late and essentially game over for the business.

Obligations of the Buyer

As the new owners coming in, they are obligated to act in the best interests of the shareholders, and they are going to want to complete due diligence to ensure they are getting what they expect.

Proposed Timetable

There are a lot of steps and actions to take, so make the time to prepare a list and then assign a delivery date. You obviously need to step through changing the directors and filings at Companies House, handing over the company authentication codes, swapping bank signatories and paying over the funds for the shares, etc...

Key clauses

These are clauses that we anticipate should be incorporated into a Shareholders Agreement, for example Compete Clauses, Drag & Tag rights and Dividend Policy.

Voluntary Departure

What happens if one of the parties drops out?

Breach

We intend the Heads of Terms to be Legally Binding in the expectation that the negotiations take an open and honest path and setting out what happens in the event of a breach.

Reserved Matters

For the sake of clarity during the purchase and subsequent handover it is important to set out what the outgoing business owner can or cannot do. For example, no new creditor arrangements, no signing commercial agreements, no control over payments to staff or directors.

Sign, Name, Position and Date

Both parties then sign this document to confirm the conversations and the accuracy of the points covered in the Heads of Terms.

For a real example please go to:

https://www.GoSellMyBusiness.com/Templates

Sale and Purchase Agreement

The sale and purchase agreement is designed to be a legally binding document and should clearly set up the terms of the sale and the handover.

The assumption we are making here is that the shares in the business are being sold. The alternative would be a business sale agreement or an asset sale agreement. In that situation, the constituent parts of the business are being broken up and each type of asset dealt with accordingly.

The Sale and Purchase Agreement sets out who are the contracting parties. It sets out exactly the number and class of shares that are being sold by whom and to whom. It specifies the amount of the proceeds and how and when they are to be paid. If there are any outstanding balances on director loan accounts or intercompany transactions, then this document is the perfect place to explain how those positions will be closed out.

As discussed in an earlier chapter, the sales of the business could be structured in any number of ways. Hence, the amount paid could be made up in a number of ways, paid over several years and even based on future Key Performance Indicator metrics. Each of these need to be clearly stipulated so as to avoid ambiguity. The last thing you want to do in 3 years is return to the document and then both parties have to interpret how that final payment was to be calculated.

As with most legal documents there should be a provision for what happens upon a breach by either party. Consider whether to include a mediator option and under which jurisdiction any possible lawsuits might be filed under.

Although the buyer is responsible for satisfying themselves that everything is in order whilst doing due diligence, they will explicitly set out here some warranties from the Seller and frequently warranties can be very extensive based on disclosure during the due diligence.

> That the Vender has made full and fair disclosure in all material respects of any matter that could reasonably be expected from the due diligence disclosure request to affect the Purchasers decision to purchase the shares on the terms set out.
>
> That the Vender has no direct or indirect interest in any company or business which has a trading relationship with, or which is likely to be or become competitive with the Company.
>
> There are no claims threatened or pending against the company by any current or past employee relating to any matter arising from or relating to the employment of the employee.
>
> The Company has not been engaged in any litigation, mediation, arbitration, dispute resolution or criminal proceedings and there are no such proceedings pending, threatened or expected, or facts or circumstances which are likely to give rise to such proceedings involving the Company.
>
> There is no outstanding order, judgment, award, or decision given by any court, tribunal, arbitrator, or regulatory body in relation to the Company.
>
> The Company is operating in accordance with all applicable laws, rules, and regulations in which it is carried on.

The above clauses are intended to help the buyer have confidence that both parties are being open and there will be no surprises once the transaction is completed. This is a legally binding document. In the event the Seller covers up or omits information on the true state of affairs then the buyer has grounds to claim compensation or even have the transaction reversed.

Other clauses to consider including:

Earn outs, Golden Handcuffs

Where a business owner wants more than a buyer is sometimes willing to pay, the Deal Structure may include an Earn Out clause linked to future performance. The way this is calculated and measured will need to be documented. Often this goes hand in hand with the outgoing business owner being asked to stay; to ensure a smooth transition to the new owners for which they are rewarded, hence the Golden Handcuffs.

Partial sale and drag and tag rights

When selling your business, you might not want to sell 100%, after all, it has been your life and baby for so long. Where there is a partial sale, a buyer might want “drag and tag” rights. This means if a buyer is found for the business the whole business can still be sold. The logic here is if either party does not think the deal is good, then they can buy the business at that price and if the deal is a good one then both should be happy to sell.

Protecting your position and any future payments (bonds, share / ownership reversion)

Some deal structures rely on deferred payments. Obviously, it is important to ensure the best chance of getting those payments. There are several ways to provide the security including Bonds, Shares and ownership reversion. Or consider setting up the deferred payments wrapped up in a loan agreement. The why is obvious. Having a legally binding loan agreement means that if the payments are not made you have clear recovery options and could even take back control of the company and then sell it again.

For a real example please go to:
https://www.GoSellMyBusiness.com/Templates

Or look at the Closing Section on our website -
https://www.GoSellMyBusiness.com/Closing

Tax efficient deal structures Business Asset Relief, Share Buy Back. Tax evasion v's Tax avoidance

This section does not constitute Tax Advice and the information was correct at time of research [Disclaimer]

There is a chapter later on about tax and offshoring. Having an idea of the end goal and structure in mind means you can ensure anything that needs to be can be included in the Sale and Purchase Agreement.

Tax Avoidance – Legal. Tax Evasion – Illegal!

It has been challenged and has been proved in the UK courts – Inland Revenue Commissioners v. Duke of Westminster (1936) "Every man is entitled, if he can, to order his affairs so that the tax attaching under the appropriate Acts is less than it otherwise would be. If he succeeds in ordering them so as to secure this result, then, however unappreciative the Commissioners of Inland Revenue or his fellow taxpayers may be of his ingenuity, he cannot be compelled to pay an increased tax."

In the UK when a business is sold the business owner is able to claim Business Asset Disposal Relief. Prior to April 2020 this was better known as Entrepreneur's relief. The bottom line is that so long as you have owned the business for 2 or more years, then you qualify for a tax charge of only 10% on the sale of the business rather than the usual Capital Gains tax percentages.

We recently structured an exit for a business owner. He was the sole shareholder. The business had £2m in cash in the bank and some other assets on the balance sheet. He was married but his wife was not a shareholder. Even though in the UK, a spouse can transfer assets to their other half in order to avoid Capital

Gains Tax on that transaction, that did not help with the two-year rule on the share ownership in place.

We will share the structure of this exit on the Go Sell My Business course. See the course outline later in this book or contact us through our website.

https://www.GoSellMyBusiness.com/ContactUs

There are additional recommendations we make on our course where properties are involved, to ensure the best structure.

Part IV: Post Sale Life

The following section does not constitute Tax Advice and the information was correct at time of research [Disclaimer].

The chances are you are not a serial entrepreneur. If you were, the chances are you have already sold a business; in which case you had an issue last time and are, as a thoroughbred problem solver, looking to avoid the same mistake again.

Having established you are probably not going to jump straight into your next business venture, you have some real soul-searching to do. What are you going to do with the rest of your life?! A true workaholic entrepreneur will have a real challenge adapting to anything other than a 70+ hour week.

This is your perfect chance to sit back, relax and think about and plan your future.

Robert Kiyosaki shared in his book, *'Rich Dad Poor Dad'*, that when he became financially independent, he did not know what to do next. He took three months off from everything. The first month was easy kicking back and relaxing and enjoying not having to do anything. Month two became boring and the third month was tough. However, he had promised himself a three-month break. This forced him to switch of and seriously think about what was really important to him and how he wanted to spend the rest of his life rather than just jump into the next thing that took his fancy. After his break for reflection months, his decision was to help others. He realised what he had learned from both his Dads; very few people had access to financial education and the benefits they would gain – hence the *Rich Dad Poor Dad* series and the Cashflow Games were born.

Being Rich is not about how much money you make, but how much money you keep, how hard it works for you and how many generations you keep it for.

Statistics show 70% of Lottery Winners lose or spend all their money in 5 years. Most people never have life changing sums of money and are used to spending what they have. Guess what, it is possible to spend a life changing sum of money and have nothing to show for it.

Don’t be one of those that say I've been running my own business for the last 20 years, but now it's time to retire. What should I do? Don’t drift. Don’t retire to a sunny climate and drift aimlessly from bar to bar on a daily basis in an alcohol induced haze. We had a holiday home in Spain and there was a community of expats that did that.

Make the most of the opportunity you have worked so hard for...

Okay, so you have not sold your business yet but by giving yourself some space and time to think and plan will ensure you make the most of the benefits of selling your business.

If you know you are potentially sitting on a Goldmine, do you know enough about wealth management, banking, off-shore accounts and how to make the most of tax havens either for sheltering the proceeds from the sales of the business or helping you keep most of the wealth once you have it?

To quote Robert Kiyosaki: “The poor and middle-class work for money. The rich have money work for them.”

So read the next set of chapters and use them to plan the chapters in your life

Chapter Thirteen: Banking

Private Banking v Private Wealth Banking

The Idea of having a private bank account at Coutts might be appealing, after all if it is good enough for the late Queen and the now King of England, then why not...?

You are hopefully about to become or will be well on your way to becoming a High Net Worth Individual. (HNWI)

The definition of a HNWI differs between the Private Banking community but is generally accepted to be they have over $1,000,000 of investible liquid assets.

JP Morgan reclassified their limits and individuals needed a minimum of $10m net assets to qualify for their Private Banking. Their other clients were moved to their Private Client Direct Program.

Private Banking will make you feel like you have arrived. You get the credit card with a name most other people only aspire to and a bank employee that will pick up the phone and talk to you at a moment's notice.

Private Wealth Banking is so much more. It is the ultimate wealth hack. It is designed by the rich, for the rich. If you are not a High Net Worth Individual, then you can not join the club.

The sooner you make getting into a Private Wealth Bank a priority, the better off you will be as you will have access to whole new world of investment opportunities that less well-off people are not allowed to access. These products will also help protect you in a down market and the returns are higher whilst the product management fees are lower than the retail market.

To get there quicker, consider paying all your earnings into your investments and live off the income that comes from your assets. This will give you the true control over making investments that generate a passive income (not the usual get rich passive income adverts you see from internet marketers).

The other way to get there is to sell your business or get yourself in the position to make small capital events that allow you to move away from an income focus.

We are not talking about the usual banks you may be aware of. We are talking about the likes of Credit Suisse, Julius Baer and UBS amongst others.

Julius Baer – minimum investment levels are now $10m of Liquid assets.

Deutsche Bank – 180-page document to complete to even be considered.

Whichever bank you ultimately consider, they will tear your whole life apart and track down every account you ever had anywhere and audit every transaction.

However, once your application has been reviewed and accepted and your account is open you get access to Lombard lending. So, what happens here is you open your Julius Baer account with $10m of investable assets. The $10m needs to be liquid and investible and held in stocks, shares, REIT's etc. You are now extended a Lombard Lending credit facility up to the $10m in case you need some cash for whatever and don't want to sell or mess with any of your existing investments. You can borrow what you need, at a low interest rate compared to normal people and for whatever purpose. You could borrow to buy additional investments or decide you want that Sunseeker Manhattan 68 with a £2.6m price tag.

So, your position looks like this: you have $10m invested via the bank. You borrow £2.6m at 1% per annum. The loan is secured against your invested portfolio. You will pay £26,000 interest per year. There is no capital repayment until you sell the boat. At that point the boat is sold, costing you £26,000 interest per year and the boat depreciation since purchase.

(Ignoring all the fuel, mooring and servicing costs). So, ask yourself, would you want to liquidate £2.6m of investments or pay £26,000 per year and settle up at the end...? For me it is a no brainer.

I have been told that you should not spend more than 10% of your net worth on a boat.

Chapter Fourteen: Tax Planning

UK Taxation and Offshore tax planning is an extremely complex area, and the relevant tax legislation is constantly changing. You should never take any action until you have spoken to a suitably qualified professional who can advise you on your particular circumstances.

You have a couple of options available to make the sale of your business tax efficient. UK tax rules for Entrepreneurs, formally Entrepreneurs Tax Relief and now Business Asset Disposal Relief or BADR, as it is abbreviated to.

The tax relief for the sale of business assets refers to persons who sell a certain part of their property and receive tax relief for it. It applies to the sale of all or part of the assets. In this case, you pay less capital gains tax when you sell your assets. Previously, tax relief on the sale of business assets was known as entrepreneur's relief and applied to capital gains of £10 million.

From March 2020 it has been capped at £1 million. Under the new guidelines, you'll no longer be entitled to the tax relief on future capital gains if you've claimed entrepreneur's relief. Suppose you want to give up your business because of retirement or the termination of your employment. In this case, the business asset disposal relief can be an excellent option for you because your business is valuable. You can get a reduction on capital gains to get more profit from your business.

The business asset disposal release is available to persons who sell all or part of their business on the following basis:

You must be the sole business partner for two years prior to the sale of the business assets.

You must've owned the business for at least 2 years.

These two conditions are necessary for you to benefit when you sell your business assets. The same conditions also apply if you don't sell the business but choose to close it down.

You must also remember that you must sell the business assets within three years in order to benefit from the relief.

The other option is moving ahead of time to a tax efficient jurisdiction. There are lots of pros and cons. Match the suitability for your lifestyle, not everyone can sit on the beach in the Seychelles and drink Pina Colada. You will need to understand and plan a long time ahead before the transaction occurs. Becoming a non domicile can take some time and commitment with many hoops to jump through, but the tax advantage makes it worthwhile.

The concept of domicile is extremely important when it comes to overseas tax planning and inheritance tax. It is important that nationality, citizenship and the colour of your passport does not necessarily dictate your domicile location. One of the most tax efficient ways of life is to become a passport nomad, with multiple golden passports, offshore banking and becoming a Non-Dom.

Chapter Fifteen: Non-Resident

You are normally domiciled in the country you refer to as your home and not the place that you may find yourself temporarily living. It is possible for someone to live in the UK for 50+ years but still be domiciled in another country. Your domicile is normally the country you class as your homeland or where you intend to die. You can be resident in multiple countries but only domiciled in one.

Your original domicile is likely to be in the country of your father at birth or if your parents are unmarried then it is your mother's domicile. You can however change your domicile and make a new country your domicile of choice. There will be domicile rules for each country but to keep this simple you can make a country a domicile of choice if you intend to stay there for the rest of your days. You would also need to cease to reside in the previous country of domicile.

There is also a domicile of dependency which only applies to children under the age of 16. Your domicile as a child will always be where your father (or mother if unmarried) resides. So, if a father changes domicile then the child's domicile changes with him. There will be exceptions to the rules in different countries, but the drag-and-tag rules pretty much apply universally.

NB. There's a UK inheritance Tax Trap of "deemed domicile" if you were resident for 17 out of the last 20 years or if you have only lost your UK domicile status within the last 3 years.

The UK residence test from 2013 looks at your UK ties, having UK accommodation, UK dependant family, or UK employment. Other things like UK Clubs, UK Banks are not included in the test. Having a UK Home will automatically make you a resident, but 'home' is not defined so having a UK property that is not your 'home' is not a residency test.

The new statutory residency test has three categories; people who will always be non-resident; people who will always be resident and people who are non-resident depending on their visits to the UK

People who are always non-resident are people who leave the UK under a long-term full-time work contract. You become non-resident from the date of departure providing you visit the UK fewer than 91 days or work in the UK for less than 30 days. A workday is classed as working more than 3 hours per day.

People who are definitely resident are people who spend 183 days or more in a tax year. You have only one home and that is in the UK. You have full-time employment in the UK. If you have an overseas property as your home, you will still be a UK resident if you spend more than 90 days in your UK home.

People who could be considered UK resident or non-resident, this will apply to most people leaving the UK. The government state the following five connection factors:

- Family – the individual's spouse, civil partner, common law equivalent, provided they are not separated from them or have minor children in the UK

- Accommodation – the individual has a UK Home

- Substantive work in the UK – the individual does substantive work in the UK but does not work in the UK Full-Time

- UK Prescence – the individual spends 90 days or more in the UK

- More time in the UK than any other country

Leavers of the UK, when someone leaves the UK there is a residency test with the scale of factors

- Fewer than 16 days they are a non-resident
- 16-45 days they are only a resident if four or more factors apply
- 46-90 days they are only a resident if three or more factors apply
- 91-120 days they are only a resident if two or more factors apply
- 121-182 days they are only a resident if one or more factors apply
- 183 days always a resident

So, to remain classed as a non-resident your limits are

- 0 connection factors – up to 182 days
- 1 connection factors – up to 120 days
- 2 connection factors – up to 90 days
- 3 connection factors – up to 45 days
- 4 connection factors – up to 15 days

A day is a deemed day over midnight, so someone arriving on a Friday and leaving on a Monday the deemed days are Friday, Saturday, Sunday. Deemed rules apply when you have 3 or more ties, have been present in the UK for more than 30 days in the tax year, and have been a UK resident in one or more of the previous three years.

HMRC have also updated their guidance on using social media for work purposes – in transit counts as a day of residence. So, someone arriving on a Friday and leaving on a Monday who uses social media for work on the Monday will now be classed as 4 deemed days.

An individual who is classed as a UK resident and domiciled in the UK is liable to UK tax on their global income and gains.

An individual who is classed as a UK resident but not UK domiciled is only liable for worldwide income or gains that are remitted to the UK

An individual who is non-resident will be liable for UK income on UK sourced income but will be exempt from UK capital gains on all assets except when used in UK Trade or UK Property.

Chapter Sixteen: Offshoring

The last chapter was primarily about Income Tax and Status. The other key tax when it comes to asset disposal is Capital Gains Tax. In order for an individual to avoid capital gains tax (CGT), they must normally be non-resident for more than five full tax years.

If you've not been resident in the UK during this time, it's still possible to avoid capital gains tax by becoming non-resident in the UK for the tax year of disposal. If you meet the five-year non-residency period and become resident in the UK again, any gains on assets disposed of while you were away from the UK will be taxed on your return to the UK. Different rules apply to the disposal of residential property than to ordinary business assets.

You have some options for countries that have zero tax. Yes, zero tax on international business capital gains. You will need to do your research on each country to see what is suitable and rules change all the time.

Anguilla

Bahamas

British Virgin Islands

Cayman Islands

Delaware USA

Marshall Islands

Mauritius

Panama

Samoa

Seychelles

St. Kitts & Nevis

St. Vincent

Ras Al Khaimah

You also have countries who have low corporate tax rates such as Cyprus with a corporate tax rate of 12.5%. Then there are countries like Belize that have no taxes for income derived from outside Belize. Like many of the offshore jurisdictions, Belize has a low incorporation cost and no public records of directors and shareholders. Like all of the offshore countries you will need an agent to act for you and a registered address if you don't want to live there. Yes, you read that correctly, you don't need to live there although having been to most of the offshore countries, there are not many nicer places in the world to kick back and relax to.

Passporting countries, golden visas, and golden passports, often referred to as 'second passports', are the result of civic participation policies, where people contribute financially to certain initiatives in a country in exchange for citizenship.

When a person applies for a golden passport, they and their immediate family receive a residence permit that can be renewed indefinitely as long as the investment in that country continues. According to the International Monetary Fund, holding a second passport offers several advantages, including the ability to travel or leave the home country without the visas required for the original passport.

More than 25 countries around the world offer these programmes for investors who want to participate in certain projects or keep an investment for a certain period of time in exchange for immigration status for themselves and their dependents. Each programme has its own standards and offers different incentives for investors. So, if you're planning to invest in a Golden Visa or Golden Passport, you should check the aspects listed below depending on your family's needs and whether you're able to meet the essential standards.

As with everything relating to taxation, domicile and requirements they are ever changing.

There are a few different ways to apply for a golden visa. The most popular way is through purchasing a foreign property (real estate), which is offered by the majority of golden passport countries. The cost of real estate ranges from $200,000 to over $2 million.

Other investing possibilities may include:

Making a capital investment in the shares/stocks of a corporation

Investing funds in the country's public debt or government bonds

Creating job opportunities

Contribute to the scientific or technical innovation of a country

Keep in mind that these investment opportunities are not available in all countries that grant Golden Visas, and each country will have different rules and requirements that frequently change.

Anguilla

Antigua and Barbuda

Austria

Bulgaria

Canada

Germany

Greece

Grenada

Ireland

Malta

New Zealand

Portugal

Singapore

Spain

St. Kitts and Nevis

St. Lucia

Switzerland

The Cayman Islands

The United Kingdom

Turkey

United Arab Emirates

United States of America

Vanuatu

There is also the option of Digital Nomad Visa's

Digital nomad visas are permits to work in countries where the applicants are staying. Like tourist visas, they're easy to obtain, but also allow longer stays. A digital nomad visa allows its holder to work during their stay in a country as long as they don't enter the local labour market. They don't compete with locals for jobs and work independently of local employers.

Each country that issues visas for digital nomads has its own policies and regulations. In some, eligible citizens can submit their application conveniently online. In others, applicants must submit their application through an embassy or consulate.

Remote workers should check the requirements and application process for a digital nomad visa in their destination country.

An applicant for a digital nomad visa usually needs:

A suitable and valid passport

Proof of a regular income from a distance

Suitable accommodation

No criminal record

In many countries where digital nomad visas are available, an application fee may also be charged.

Travellers should always check whether they need additional documents such as health insurance, vaccination certificates or other health requirements and covid restrictions.

Anguilla

Antigua & Barbuda

Argentina

Aruba

Australia

Barbados

Belize

Bermuda

Brazil

Cambodia

Cape Verde

Cayman Islands

Colombia

Costa Rica

Croatia

Curacao

Cyprus

Czech Republic

Dominica

Dubai, UAE

Ecuador

Estonia

Georgia

Germany

Greece

Grenada

Iceland

Indonesia

Italy

Jamaica

Malta

Mauritius

Mexico

Montenegro

Montserrat

Norway

Panama

Portugal

Romania

Serbia

Seychelles

Spain

Sri Lanka

St. Lucia

Taiwan

Thailand

Vietnam

Each country is different, Argentine authorities introduced a special visa for remote workers on 21 May 2022. The Argentine Digital Nomad Visa allows digital nomads to work remotely for an international or Argentine company.

The Rentista visa for digital nomads in Costa Rica allows its holder to stay in the country for up to two years, with the possibility of extending it. It's intended for small investors who want to offer their services in Costa Rica. Although you need to prove a regular income of $2,500 USD per month, it's not difficult to get the visa.

If you want to live in Portugal as a digital nomad, you can apply for a D7 passive income visa, which is very similar to the Costa Rican Rentista visa. The main requirement is that you've to prove you have sufficient income and where this money comes from. With this visa, you can stay in Portugal for one year and then renew it for two years at a time. After five years in Portugal on a D7 passive income visa, you can apply for a residence permit if you pass a Portuguese language test.

The Maltese digital nomad visa is initially for one year but can be extended up to three years. You need to have accommodation which can be rented at €12,000 per year and an income of €2,500 per month, and valid medical cover. After 182 days in a tax year you can then apply for a golden visa program Global Residency Program. This has zero tax on foreign income and no inheritance tax. You do need to pay €15,000 per year in local tax and the program takes about 6 months to process. The main advantages of Malta are they are English speakers, drive on the left, fibre-optic internet, a great climate all year round, a great health service, and the business and economy are all based on English law. The nomad visa costs about €300, and you get a digital ID card for visa-free travel around Europe.

Every country has its advantages and with the digital nomad visa, if you don't like the country, you can move on to another, and another, and another…

The last three chapters are not designed to give you advice or encourage you to pack a suitcase. They are there to get you to think of the possibilities and if you have a desire to head for the beaches or hills, then you might want to explore not only those climates but also looking to optimise the financial benefits of planning ahead.

You only make money when you sell your business

Richard Branson in his autobiography, Losing My Virginity, admitted that when running Virgin Records it was tough, cashflow was a challenge and he was in the position that he had to decide who to pay or find additional funds. He made his money when he sold the business to Thorn EMI for £510m.

What was also interesting to note is it was his baby, and his employees were more like friends. It hit him hard as he felt he had sold them out. Blood, Sweat and Tears.

Deborah Meaden, well known for her appearances on Dragons' Den, made £33 million selling her stake in Weststar Holidays when a partial exit was negotiated with Phoenix Equity Partners.

Business owners and Entrepreneurs sell their businesses for any number of reasons. For some it could be they want to take a back seat and enjoy the fruits of their labour or spend more time with their families and friends. Others have found the next 'shiny object' that has grabbed their attention and will drive their passion for excitement and new challenges forward. For others they may have preferred the variety and challenges of a start-up rather than pushing the business on.

Now what should I do?

We have put together a course that compliments and builds on all the concepts in this book.

The course is designed for SME business owners to fully educate themselves and prepare everything needed for a possible sale. We also go into more detail of the steps and offer plenty of practical advice backed up by real life case study examples.

For those who subsequently decide they want to sell their business, in addition to ourselves we have a list of investors who are continually on the lookout for SME businesses.

To see the Agenda and Register for the next course

https://www.GoSellMyBusiness.com/Course

Bibliography

Branson, Richard (1998) Losing my Virginity: The Autobiography

Kiyosaki, Robert and Lechter, Sharon (1997) Rich Dad Poor Dad, Warner Books

Hadnum, Lee, (2017) Non-Resident and Offshore Tax Planning

Hadnum, Lee (2014) Where to Base your Offshore Company

Priestly, Dan (2017) 24 Assets: Create a digital, scalable, valuable and fun business that will thrive in a fast-changing world. Rethink Press

Jeremy Harbour & Callum Laing (2016) Agglomerate: From Idea to IPO in 12 months. Rethink Press

Private banking - Wikipedia

Business Asset Disposal Relief: Eligibility - GOV.UK (www.gov.uk)

A Gift For You

We hope you have enjoyed this book. We have wanted to write it for a long time. We planned it several years ago before we actually sat down and wrote it. However, a worldwide pandemic got in the way and one of us decided to change countries.

Throughout the book you will find references to various templates and cheat sheets to help you sell your business, create valuations and present your business for sale. Included in the templates, which cost tens of thousands of pounds to create, are a number of topics covered to help you ultimately prepare everything you need to do to sell your business.

Depending on when you read this, the templates may have been updated and added to. If you are a subscriber then you will automatically receive notification of an update.

Within the templates are a few examples of the critical sales brochure and your Information Memorandum. If you are not confident in putting together this document, we have a done-for-you service where one of our consultants can do this for you.

We have also put together online videos and instructions on how to use the templates. But if, like me, you prefer to attend a live class and share with like-minded people, you can also attend a classroom event.

We also have a virtual dating agency, where you can market your business and get matched together with people from around the world that are looking to buy businesses just like yours. Even if you are not ready to fully list the business for sale, we have a pre-listing option where we can start matching buyers who are interested in your sector ready for when your Information Memorandum and data room are ready.

There is also the option of having your due diligence data room all set up and made for you, ready to be shared with the prospective buyers of your business.

If you sell your business and let Mark know, he will invite you to his private members' wine club in London to treat you and chat to you about your sale, wine, and what's next in the great universe!

https://www.GoSellMyBusiness.com/Templates